S. R. Stoddard

Lake George and Lake Champlain

A Book of to-day

S. R. Stoddard

Lake George and Lake Champlain
A Book of to-day

ISBN/EAN: 9783337146368

Printed in Europe, USA, Canada, Australia, Japan

Cover: Foto ©ninafisch / pixelio.de

More available books at **www.hansebooks.com**

AND

LAKE CHAMPLAIN.

A BOOK OF TO-DAY.

BY

S. R. STODDARD.

INDEX.
Lake George and Lake Champlain.

A. C. A 109
Adams Landing..... 139
Advert'm'ts Indexed. 145
Alburgh Springs..... 140
Assembly Point..... 35
Au Sable Chasm..... 113
Baldwin............. 77
Bloody Pond........ 20
Bixby, Dr. George F. 137
Bluff Pt.......128, 167
Fulwaga Bay........ 104
Burlington.......... 112
Camp Life........... 3
Camp Watson....... 141
Carillon............. 102
Cedar Beach........ 109
Champlain's Battle.. 98
Colchester Point..... 113
Crown Point Ruins.. 108
Cumberland Head... 136
Down the Lake..... 29
Eagle Camp......... 139
Essex............... 101
Fishing............. 6

Forts.
Cassin.............. 98
Gage................ 19
George.............. 10
Montgomery........ 138
St. Frederick....... 102
Ticonderoga (Ruins) 98
Wm. Henry (Ruins) 9
French Point........ 57
Glens Falls.......... 21
Business Cards, 147,151
Gordon's Landing.. 138
Great Back Bay..... 140
Grog Harbor........ 107
Hague............... 71
Highgate Springs.... 143
Howe's Landing..... 79
Hulett's Landing.... 63

Hotels (Advertisements, indexed.. 145
Albion............... 37
Bolton House....... 49
Burleigh House..... 82
Carpenter House... 14
Central Hotel...... 13
Champlain,
 (Bluff Point)..128, 167
Champl'n (Maquam) 143
Crosbyside 15
Cumberland House 134
R. L. George House 36
Fort Wm. Henry H. 11
Fouquet House..... 134
Fourteen Mile I... 51-B
Gibbs House........ 105
Grove Hotel........ 36
Hillside House..... 72
Horicon Lodge..... 36
Hulett's Landing H. 63
Hundred Island H. 51-C
Island Harbor...... 73
Kattskill House.... 37

Hotels—continued.
Keneeaw..........51-B
Kenmore 171
Lake House........ 12
L. View H., L. Geo. 41
L. View, AuSbl Csm 119
Marion House..... 39
Mohican House..15, 158
Pearl Point........ 54
Phœnix Hotel..... 71
Prospect Mt. House 14
Rising House...... 72
Rockwell House... 22
Rogers' Rock Hotel 76
Sagamore, The...49, 159
Samson's L.V'w H. 142
Saranac L'ke House 165
St. Hubert's Inn... 164
Silver Bay......... 69
Stevens House..... 108
Trout House....... 72
Trout Pavilion.... 36
Van Ness House... 113
Welden, The....... 142
Westport Inn..... 105
Willsborough, The 109
Indian Kettles...... 67

Islands.
As-You-Were...... 56
Burnt.............. 56
Canoe.............. 33
Crab............... 132
Crown.............51-A
Diamond........... 32
Dome.............. 40
Elizabeth.......... 37
Floating Battery.. 59
Four Brothers..... 110
Fourteen Mile..... 51
Half-way........... 59
Harbor 60
Hen and Chickens 51-C
Isle LaMotte....... 139
Juniper............ 110
Long............... 33
Mother Bunch..... 59
North Hero........ 139
Oahu..............51-A
Phantom.......... 55
Phelps............. 50
Prisoner's......... 77
Recluse 40
Scotch Bonnett.... 79
South Hero........ 139
Tea 29
Three Sirens...... 59
Turtle 55
Valcour............ 126
Vicar's............. 62
Ladd's Landing.... 139
Lake Champlain.... 93
 Islands............. 137
Lake George
 Discovery........ 6-A
 Business Cards.... 157

Maps.
L. Champlain and L.
 George. In front cover
Lake George Hotels
 Frontispiece.
Ticonderoga....... 81
Ticonderoga Ruins. 100
Missisquoi Park..... 144

Mountains.
Anthony's Nose.... 70
Black.............. 57
Buck.............. 39
Deer's Leap....... 63
Elephant.......... 66
Hog's Back........ 64
Prospect.......... 14
Rogers' Rock..... 76
Split Rock........ 107
Tongue...........51-B
Twin.............. 66
Old Stone Store... 14
Otter Creek....... 108
Outfit............. 3
Paradise Bay..... 56
Plattsburgh....... 133
 Battle of........ 132
Port Henry....... 104
Port Kent........ 113
Roads and Drives... 18
Rock Dunder..... 111
Roger's Slide..... 75
Rouse's Point..... 137

Railroads.
Au Sable Chasm... 113
Chateaugay....175, 174
Delaware & Hudson 173
Fitchburgh........ 175
Hudson River..... 172
Sabbath Day Point. 66
Sacrificial Stone.... 17
St. Albans......... 143
St. Mary's of the Lake 81
Saratoga—Reverse of
 book, indexed.
Shelburne Harbor... 111
South Hero 138
Split Rock 107

Steamboats.
Chateaugay........ 106
Horicon........... 16
Hudson River..... 163
Island Queen..... 17
Ticonderoga...... 17
Vermont.......... 97
Water Lily....... 105
Ticonderoga, Falls.. 81
Names............. 101
Fort............... 98
Village............ 81
Valcour, Battle of.. 127
Westport.......... 105
Whitehall......... 96
Williams' Monument 20
Willsborough Point.. 109

LAKE GEORGE.

AKE GEORGE! How the heart bounds and the pulse quickens at sound of the words that bring with them thoughts of the "Holy Lake." In fancy we again breathe the air, heavy with the odor of pines and cedar, or fragrant with the breath of blossoming clover. Again we wander among the daisies and buttercups that gem the hillside sloping so gently down to where the wavelets kiss the white beach, or floating among the verdant islands, watch the sunlight and shadow chase each other up the mountain side, while every crag and fleecy cloud is mirrored in the quiet waters below.

A memory of the past comes to me as I write; of good old days now past and gone; of lumbering coaches where now go swiftly glancing trains; of six horse tally-hos, now crowded out by monsters breathing fire and smoke; of sounding plank in place of shining ribs of steel. More comfortable now it is undoubtedly with its luxurious palace cars but the poetry has gone with the dear old stages, and the new things of the age have made living commonplace at last. The memory remains, however, of the stage of old, with its overhanging load of pleasure seekers in brave attire, suggestive of some huge bouquet of gaily colored flowers, rocking and swaying from side to side as it bowls merrily along through the shaded streets and out across the plain, creeping up the long hill, then down into the valley on the other side, where ragged urchins pelt us with great, creamy pond lilies ; of the stop at the Half-Way House, where thirsty ones partake of cooling drinks such as Brown alone can make; of the rapidly changing views as with swinging gait we cover the winding forest road ; of Williams' Monument and Bloody Pond ; and of the moment when the woods are left behind and the " Lake of the Blessed Sacrament " lies before us, green-walled at the sides and stretching away to where the rugged Tongue and misty Black Mountain close across the sparkling way.

Rightfully and becomingly does Lake George wear the proud title " Queen of American Waters." Lying along the south-eastern margin of the great Adirondacks it combines the grandure of its widest mountain lakes with the quiet loveliness of its peaceful valleys. The graceful foliage of Keene Valley, the rounded headlands of the queenly Raquette, the repose of stately Placid, the rugged grandeur of dark Avalanche, have each their counterpart here, all blended in one grand harmonious whole.

Its water of marvelous purity has a distinctive color of its own. The Raquette River flows red, the Opalescent amber; Lake George is, in its shaded depths, a positive green. Its tributary streams are few and short,—spring-born in the enwrapping hills. It is itself but a great overflowing spring in its hollow of verdure-covered rock. Its surface is 346 feet above tide and 247 feet above Lake Champlain into which, at the north, with many a wild leap and rapid race, it empties. Islands rear themselves in solitary grandeur, or are gathered in dainty clusters on its face. Of old it was said there was an island for every day in the year, and an additional mysterious, illusive, little sprite of a one that appeared only in the years divisible by four, but the unimaginative survey of 1880 proved that there are but 220 including every considerable rock around which the water breaks.

During July and August, Lake George teems with nomadic life in all its varied forms. Vagrant communities appear and disappear as if by magic; white tents gleam among the dark-green foliage, and lonely islands are suddenly astir with busy throngs. Its wilderness solitudes for the time resound with joyous shoutings, as of boys let loose from school; its rocks are flecked with blue and gray; its tree tops blush with bunting, while the very shores put on a flannelly hue, and shadowy points blossom out in duck and dimity. It is safe to say that in the course of the season a thousand people taste the pleasures and overcome the difficulties of actual camp life at Lake George.

The camp outfit should include a light axe, long-handled frying-pan, tin pail for water or coffee, tin plates, pint cups, knives and forks and fishing tackle. A stove-top laid on a fire-place of stones and mud, and supplied with one length of stove pipe will be appreciated by the cook; spruce boughs for a bed, with rubber blanket, to guard against possible, dampness, and two or three good woolen blankets for covering, will be found very comfortable. A small bag to fill with leaves or moss for a pillow, pays for itself in one night. Flannel or woolen clothing, with roomy shoes and a soft felt hat, is ordinarily the safest dress.

Ladies, wear what you have a mind to (you will, any way), but let me respectfully suggest that it be mostly flannel, with good strong shoes under foot, and a man's felt hat over head—take the man along, too, if you want to, he will be useful to row you about, take the fish off your hook, run errands, etc.

Boats and provisions may be obtained at almost any of the hotels. Bacon, salt pork, bread and butter, Boston crackers, tea, coffee, sugar, pepper and salt, with a tin box or two for containing the same are among the things needed. Milk can be obtained regularly at the farm houses, berries picked almost anywhere; ice is a luxury which may be contracted for and thrown from the passing steamers daily; a hole in the ground with a piece of bark over it forms a very good ice box; a drinking cup of leather, to carry in the pocket, comes handy at times; broad-brimmed straw hats are a nuisance. Whiskey is unnecessary, a damage and disgrace to the party; if you take it habitually to prevent colds, don't come. Colds are never taken here by sleeping out under the stars, and there is little in God's pure air and sunshine in keeping with the degrading stuff.

A shanty made of boughs will answer, in absence or anything better. It sounds well when you talk about "roughing it," but is unsatisfactory in practice. A tent may be made comfortable with the outlay of a little time and work. There are clubs who own fishing boxes or shanties, more or less rough in construction, some made simply of rough boards, with bunks for sleeping in, and with chairs, tables, stoves, etc. Some of them can be hired, the price being from $12 to $20 per week, including the use of a boat or two and in many cases a well filled ice house. The poorest cottage is an improvement on the best of tents in stormy weather.

The question of the right of individuals to acquire and hold possession of certain islands belonging to the State is somewhat complicated and as yet unsettled. The law says; "*The lands now or hereafter constituting the forest preserve shall be forever kept as wild forest lands.*" A number of these islands are occupied by responsible parties who were appointed custodians by the land commissioners, and who in good faith expended considerable money in beautifying and making these islands comfortable for summer occupancy. Their rights are respected by the public generally and their removal a question of time.

The Forest Commission, having charge of the forest preserve, was created by Chapter 283 of the laws of 1885. The forest warden, forest inspectors, foresters and other persons acting upon the forest preserve under the written employment of the forest warden, or of the Forest Commission, may, without warrant, arrest any person found upon the forest preserve violating any provisions of the act creating the commission. The Forest Commission has the same power to bring action for trespass and to recover damages for injury, or to prevent injury to the preserve which any owner of lands would be entitled to bring. The fire wardens have power to call upon any person in the territory in which they act for assistance in suppressing fires, and every person refusing to act when so called shall be liable to a fine of not less than five nor more than twenty dollars. Any person who shall willfully or negligently set fire to any forest lands belonging to the State, shall be liable to a fine of not less than fifty or more than five hundred dollars, or to imprisonment of not less than thirty days nor more than six months.

The islands of Lake George belong to the State and under existing laws, cannot be purchased, except the following: Tea, Diamond, Canoe, long, Elizabeth, Three Brothers, Dome, Recluse, Belvoir, Hiawatha, Leontine, Green, Crown, Fourteen Mile, Flora, Turtle and Harbor Islands.

Good fishing can be had at Lake George in its proper season by one possessed of a proper knowledge of the best ground. This knowledge is purchasable and can be had by the employment of competent fishermen, who furnish boat and bait also, at about $3 per day. The game fish are the lake trout and black bass. The trout are usually taken by deep trolling early in the season and with live bait in deep water, later. Black bass are caught by trolling or still fishing over rocky ground. Rock bass and perch abound on certain well-known ledges while the plebian "bull-head" flourishes on the softer bottom. This last fish, although not considered good in many waters is here firm of flesh and palatable. Brook trout fishing makes a fair return for labor expended, the yield in the various streams emptying into the lake being in ratio to the whipping they get. Here the various "flies" that are comparatively valueless for lake fishing may be used to advantage.

Hunting is little considered here although the woods yield a fair share of birds and small game and deer are not uncommon in the mountains along the narrows.

The existence of Lake George was first made known to Europeans in 1609, through the writings of Samuel de Champlain. It was known to the Indians as Andia-to-roc-te (place where the lake contracts). Champlain went no further south than the falls at Ticonderoga.

In the month of August, 1642, a war party of Iroquois, returning from Canada to their homes in the Mohawk Valley, passed through Lake George with three prisoners, tortured, maimed and bleeding. They were a French Jesuit, Father Jogues, Rene Goupil and Guillame Couture, the first white men known to have seen the "Lake of the Blessed Sacrament."

Again, on the 29th of May, 1646, Father Jogues, with Sieur Bourden, engineer in chief on the governor's staff, and six friendly Indians arrived at the outlet on the eve of the festival of Corpus Christi, and in commemoration of the day they named it the "Lake of the Blessed Sacrament." For over a hundred years it bore its beautiful name of *Lac Du St. Sacrament*, then, in 1755, General Johnson encamped at its head and called it *Lake George*, in honor of George the Second, and then reigning king of Great Britain.

"*Horican*," the "Silvery Water," was simply a fancy of Cooper's. He says: "It occurred to me that the French name of this lake was too complicated, the American too common-place, and the Indian too unpronounceable for either to be used familiarly in a work of fiction,"* so he called it "Horican." The name has been generally accepted as historical

---
* "The last of the Mohicans." Introduction to edition of 1831. New York George P. Putnam.

and advanced by admirers as one more indication of the poetic temperament and appreciation of the beautiful fitness of things possessed by the noble red man. It is not explained, however, why, in these later days, Cooper's creation is accepted as the *name*, while his spelling is ignored.

Isaac Jogues, who first saw, and seeing, wrote of Lake George, was born at Orleans, Jan. 10, 1607; entered the Jesuit Society at Rouen, 1624, and three years later removed to the college of La Fletche. He completed his divinity studies at Clermont College, Paris, and was ordained Priest in February, 1636. In the spring of that year he embarked as a missionary for Canada, arriving early in July, and soon proceeded to his far-away station on the Otawa river in the land of the Hurons. On his return from Quebec where he came for supplies in 1642, he was captured with his party and carried through Lake George to the Mohawk, suffering torture at that and various other times. The following year, in July, he made his escape by aid of the Dutch at Ft. Orange, who sent him to France, where he arrived about Christmas, and was received with great honor and reverence. In 1644 he returned to Canada, and in 1646 returned by the old route to his former masters, the Mohawks, a missionary from his superior, and an ambassador for the French nation, to ratify a treaty with the savages. Once more he returned to Canadà, and once more passed over the holy lake to his "Mission of the Martyrs," where on his arival he was met by torture and paid the penalty of his zeal with his pure devoted self sacrificing life.

In 1609, Hendrick Hudson ascended the North river to its junction with the Mohawk, and the same year Champlain sailed as far south as Ticonderoga, on the lake which now bears his name. At that time the *Algonquins* occupied the land north of the St. Lawrence, and the Five Nations (a powerful confederacy, consisting of the *Mohawks, Oneidas, Onondagas, Cayugas,* and *Senecas*), were gathered in the valley of the Mohawk. The tribes of the north and south were continually at war with each other. The land between the St. Lawrence and the Mohawk was debatable ground, and the country along the shores of St. Sacrament and Champlain was a solitude, for the lakes, stretching north and south, formed a pathway through the wilderness, over which savage nations were constantly going to war against each other. This had driven all who were inclined to occupy the land beyond the mountains; and presumably this is why it received its Indian name, signifying "the lake that is the gate of the country."

The English secured their right to the country claimed by the Five Nations by virtue of a treaty with that people; the French claimed it by right of Champlain's discovery. Both nations aimed to keep the friendship of the Indian tribes, in which the French met with the greater success. They were constantly extending their lines, and sending over zealous missionaries and enterprising traders, who carried glass beads, fire-water, and the bread of life to the red man, and created a great revival of religion among them, in consequence of which a good many English scalps were taken.

In 1731 the French advanced to Crown Point

and built a fort, which they called "St. Frederick." The slow English remonstrated, but took no active measures to resist the advance on what they claimed as their territory. The Indians that gathered around the French fort were a constant menace to the exposed home of the English settlers of the upper Hudson, and often was the story told of a sudden descent on some unprotected point, a rifle shot, a gleaming knife or bloody tomahawk, and a retreat by the light of a burning building. In the words of the French concerning their Indian allies, they occasionally "struck a blow and returned with some scalps."

In time the English realized that something more effective than protests would be needed to resist the encroachment of the French, and in 1755 General, afterward Sir William, Johnson was dispatched to take charge of the little affair. He arrived at the head of Lac du St. Sacrament August 28th, and at once renamed the lake, calling it Lake George, in honor of the then reigning King of Great Britain. Not content with this hydraulic victory he issued a proclamation, in which he said: "I propose to go down this lake with a part of the army, and take post at the end of it, at a pass called 'Ticonderogue,' there to await the coming up of the rest of the army, and then attack Crown Point." While General Johnson was waiting to note the effect of his proclamation, the Baron Dieskau, with 1,400 men, 600 of whom were Indians, advanced, September 8th, to attack Fort Lyman, now Fort Edward. When within four miles of the fort, the Indians refused to proceed further, it is thought from their known fear of cannon. Dieskau then turned the head of his little army toward Lake George, and had reached the place where Williams' monument now stands, when news was brought that the English were advancing toward them. Forming an ambush in shape of a hollow square, open toward the north; the points extending on each side of the road, the French awaited the coming of the enemy, which soon appeared—1,000 English and 200 Indians—under Col. Ephraim Williams and old King Hendrick. It happened that among Dieskau's Indians were some of the great league of the Iroquois, who, seeing that the English were accompanied by a party of their sworn friends, fired guns in the air as a warning, and, by this act, turned what might have been the annihilation of the detachment into simply a bad defeat. The French opened fire, at once. Colonel Williams and King Hendrick fell, and their followers retreated, followed by the French. The noise of the engagement was heard at Lake George, and a force of 300 was dispatched to the assistance of the English, while breastworks of fallen trees were thrown up with all haste in front of the camp. Soon came the English in confusion, closely pursued by the French. The guns of the English could not be brought to bear, without injuring friend and foe alike, and it appeared to be Dieskau's object to keep thus close on the heels of the retreating English, and enter the fortified camp with them; but as, with joyful shouts, the survivors tumbled over the logs among their friends, they, with wonder, beheld the French halt while the Indian allies skulked in the swamps. The pause was for a few minutes only, but it afforded the English time to perfect their plans of defense, and, when the French did finally advance, they were received by a well-worked battery against which they could not prevail. The attack was spirited, and the defense stubborn. The engagement began a little before noon, and lasted until about four o'clock, when the enemy retreated, and the English took their turn at pursuit. Dieskau was wounded and taken prisoner, dying afterward, it is said, from the effect of his wounds. Johnson was also wounded early in the day, and the command devolved on General Lyman, who behaved with unexceptionable bravery throughout the entire engagement.

The French loss, killed and wounded, was nearly 400 men; the English about 300. Johnson, having earned glory enough, spent the remainder of the season in building Fort William Henry.

In March, 1757, Vaudreuil, with 1,500 French and Indians, came over the ice to attack Fort William Henry. The attack was made at two o'clock on the morning of the 19th, but the garrison was apprised of the enemy's approach and repulsed him successfully. He succeeded, however, in burning a number of sloops and batteaux, that were frozen in the ice, in front of the fort.

Early in August, following Vaudreuil's unsuccessful attack, the Marquis de Montcalm, with nearly 8,000 French and Indians, advanced on Fort William Henry. Colonel Monro was then in command of the fort. He withstood the siege for six days in hopes of relief from General Webb; but, receiving none, sent a messenger to Montcalm stating the terms on which he would surrender. The terms were substantially that the English should be allowed to march out with the honors of war, carrying arms and baggage. They were agreed to, and at noon the next day the English marched over to the entrenched camp, there to remain until the following morning, leaving the sick and wounded under the protection of the French general. But, even while they were passing out, the

Indians swarmed in through the embrasures, attacking the sick and helpless. The horrible scenes that followed are thus described by Father Robaud in his "Relations:" "I saw one of these barbarians come forth out of the casements, which nothing but the most insatiate avidity for blood could induce him to enter, for the infected atmosphere which exhaled from it was insupportable, carrying in his hand a human head, from which streams of blood were flowing, and which he paraded as the most valuable prize he had been able to seize."

In the morning, when the English marched out of the entrenched camp, and, protected by *three hundred* French, the insufficiency of their escort became apparent. The savages swarmed in the woods on every side, and hung like a dark storm-cloud along their path. Low, ominous muttering, like distant thunder, came from the surging crowd, rising higher and higher, until, with fierce yells, they fell on the panic-stricken English, and struck them down in the face of their helpless guard. Soon all semblance of order ceased, the march changing into a selfish race for life. The butchery, which at first was the work of a few, became general; the savages murdered helpless women and children, and tore men from the ranks, and, like wild beasts, fought among themselves for the sickening prize of a human scalp.

It is difficult to exonerate Montcalm from all blame, for he knew the nature of the savages, and their treatment of the sick and wounded in the old fort the day before, and still, with 6,000 French at command, sent only 300 to protect a long line of men, women, and children from wild beasts, thirsting for their blood. The number that perished is unknown, but has been estimated by some as high as 1,500.

Their object accomplished, the French returned north, leaving the fort a heap of smouldering ruins, and the bones of the English bleaching in the sun.

Another act in the great drama of the Lake. A

year has passed away, and the curtain rises on a scene of wondrous beauty. The same old mountains slope down, amphitheater-like, around the lake; the mists of midsummer hang over the land; martial music fills the air. The sound of bugles and of highland pipes echo from the mountain side, and a thousand boats, bearing 15,000 men, in all the varied colors of royal court, of clan and forest, with banners waving, and hearts beating high with hope, move away down the glassy lake.

Thus, on the morning of July 5th, 1758, Abercrombie embarked and sailed to the attack of Fort Ticonderoga. On the following day, at Trout-Brook, Lord Howe fell, and the evening of the 9th saw the inglorious return of the defeated army.

The following year Amherst passed the same way, capturing Ticonderoga and Crown Point, and driving the French into Canada.

Fort William Henry is described as square, built of pine logs covered with sand, flanked by bastions at the four corners, and surrounded by a deep ditch. The ruins are in the sandy, tree-covered bluff west of the railroad depot, between it and the Fort William Henry Hotel. The outline is still preserved, showing the form of the old fort, nearly square, flanked on the west, south, and a part of the east side, by a ditch, and on the north by the lake. The "Old Fort Well" still remains near the east side, partially filled with stones and rubbish. Just where the fence which now incloses the grounds on the east would run, if continued out into the lake, deep under water, is the old Fort dock. Beyond the dock a little way, may be seen, on a still day, the

FORT GEORGE.

charred remains of an old hulk, with blackened ribs and keel half hidden in the sand, supposed to have been one of the number sunk by Vaudreuil in February, 1757. Shell and cannon balls have been taken from it at different times, and in 1820 two small cannon were removed from the wreck.

FORT GEORGE is a half-mile east of old Fort William Henry, back on the low bluff, around which the railroad swings as it turns away from the lake. It was built in 1759, by General Amherst, the portion completed being but a bastion of what was then designed for an extensive fortification. It was occupied as a military post while the necessity for one lasted. Commanded (!) in 1775 by Capt. John Nordberg, "in a little cottage as a Hermit where I was very happy for six months;" taken possession of by Col. Bernard Romans, May 12 (two days after the capture of Ticonderoga by Ethan Allen), and held by the Americans until the close of the Revolution. It is now but a great heap of earth, sloping off from the edge to toward the centre and north held in place by the walls, which are quite well preserved on the east side. The greater portion of the stonework has been removed, and burned into lime.

On the table land, a little to the southwest of the fort, was the old entrenched camp, the scene of Dieskau's defeat by General Johnson in 1755.

FORT WILLIAM HENRY HOTEL, William Noble owner and proprietor, H. P. C. Johnson, manager. Post Office, Lake George. Capacity 600. Rates $4,00 to $5.00 per day according to room.

The original Fort William Henry Hotel was built in the year 1854-5 by a stock company, of which Thomas Thomas was president, and opened for guests in June of the last named year, with Daniel Gale as manager. The architect was a son of the president of the company, the builder Franklin M. Wright of Glens Falls. The original structure had a front of 200 feet with a wing extending backward from its centre 130 feet, and was four stories high with basement. In 1855 and the spring of 1856 the front was extended towards the east making it as it now stands with a total frontage of 334 feet. In 1865 Daniel Gale and A. C. Joselin purchased the property of the company, Mr. Gale succeeding as sole owner and proprietor two years later and continuing in the management until August, 1868, when he sold it to T. Roessle & Son of Albany, for $125,000. During the following winter and spring the house was remodeled at a cost of about $200,000. The entire structure was raised 26 feet making room for the basement and main story, the latter with ceilings 16 feet high. A mansard roof was also added making the building seven stories high. On February, 1891, Mr. William Noble of the Grenoble Flats, New York city, purchased the property of T. E. Roessle the surviving partner.

The space between the house and depot is rich in history and tradition and was once the centre of vast military operations which brought together a host four times greater than could now find quarters in all the hotels and cottages along Lake George's teem ing shores. Now, winding paths lead to the water, and stately pines grow on the ramparts and in the trenches, where, of old, men watched for the savage foe or made merry around the barrack fire.

The Lake House, H. E. Nichols, proprietor, is on the west shore between the water and the main street of the little village of Caldwell. Capacity 300. Open June 1st.

This is one of the oldest houses of Lake George and is firmly established in the hearts of many who are as regular in their appearance as the seasons. The office always impresses a new comer with the idea that he has unexpectedly dropped in while a

LAKE HOUSE, LAKE GEORGE, N. Y.

reception is in progress, as it is a favorite gathering place for the lady guests of the house. It is attractive with tasteful decorations and a paneled ceiling of native woods, while an ample fireplace, ornate in terra cotta, gives promise of a cheery comfort of a chilly evening in early spring or late summer when a fire may be a welcome addition.

Within the office is telegraph office and a desk

with pictures, books, and periodicals. The piazzas, back and front, give choice of position at different hours of the day. All along the front extends a double line of thick-leaved maples, under and through which is displayed a charmingly restful view of village, church and mountain. On the east a shaded lawn slopes down to the water's edge. On the grounds are four comfortable cottages, two of which, standing at the lake shore, with balconies that almost overhang the waters, are fine specimens of architecture. Excursion steamers and the regular line boats all land at the dock.

Mr. Nichols, the proprietor, is well known to Lake George visitors, having served here in the capacity of clerk and general manager for some time. He is energetic and thorough and will undoubtedly hold the Lake House where it has stood so long, a favorite among Lake George visitors. North of the Lake House is the Warren County Court House and jail. South of the Lake House is a large private boarding house kept by Mrs. J. Quinlan; rates, $8 to $10 per week; will accommodate 25.

CENTRAL HOTEL is just north of the Lake House, on the opposite side of the main street. It is substantial, comfortable, and attractive, and is open summer and winter. An omnibus, free to guests, runs to all trains and boats. Board $2 per day; $8 to $14 per week. Capacity of house 100.

The "Central" opens under new management this year — that of Stewart D. Brown, son of the veteran George Brown, whose name has been associated with the hotel business of Lake George and French Mountain for nearly half a century. The new proprietor in addition to a considerable experience, brings youthful push and energy into the business and will no doubt add laurels to the name. The house shows marked signs of modern ideas as a result of the general overhauling and re-arrange-

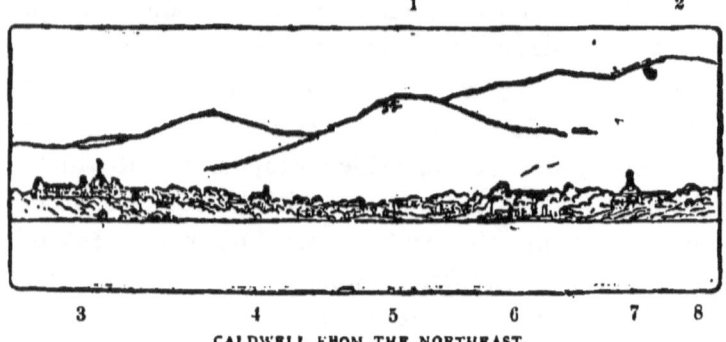

CALDWELL FROM THE NORTHEAST.

1 Rattlesnake Cobble; 2 Prospect Mountain House; 3 Fort William Henry Hotel; 4 R. C. Church; 5 Carpenter House; 6 Lake House; 7 Court House and Jail; 8 Central House.

ment for summer guests presenting a handsome appearance from office to kitchen.

The Arlington, just south of the Central House, J. T. Bryant, proprietor, will accommodate about 60.

CARPENTER HOUSE, J. H. Carpenter, proprietor. Capacity, 70. Rates, $2 per day; $7 to $10 per week. This house is still further south and directly opposite the old stone store. It is neat and orderly, and will accommodate about 70 guests. A free stage runs to trains and boats.

PROSPECT MOUNTAIN rises west of the village, its top less than a mile in an air line from where steamer and cars exchange their crowds of passengers. The Mount Ferguson House at the top will, presumably, furnish refreshments and accommodations as heretofore.

"THE OLD STONE STORE," on the east side of Main Street, opposite the Carpenter House, is a venerable landmark, known for years, and of general interest for its unique collection of Japanese goods and curios, its photographs and books, stationery and artists' materials; to the lover of a good cigar for its collection of various brands from Park & Tilford, and to young people generally as headquarters for fine chocolate and mixed candies. It also contains a drug and prescription department in care of M. Asher, Ph.G., of New York. The proprietor is Dr. W. J. Hunt, a young man of sterling qualities, popular with resident and visitor, and with a gratifying and steadily growing practice.

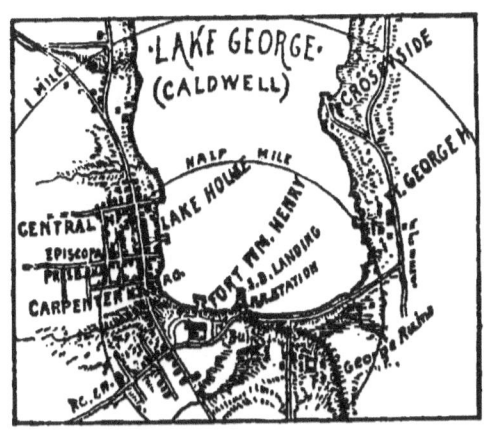

D. T. Sands, one door north of the old Stone Store, is a young merchant of promise and worthy of patronage. His specialty is fancy goods, dress goods, and ladies' shoes.

C. A. & E. J. West, on the west side of the street need no commendation. They are a solid firm and deal in solid goods, staple and fancy, with unlimited groceries and canned goods. Camping parties will do well to make a note of this.

THE POST OFFICE is on the west side of the street, a short distance north of the Central Hotel.

THE CROSBYSIDE is on the east shore opposite the Lake House. Capacity of house and cottages about 200. Rates given on application. R. C. Jenkins, manager. Steamers land at the dock and an omnibus conveys guests to and from all trains Telegraph in the office.

Cottages noticeably prominent along shore, north of Crosbyside, belong severally to Mrs. M. S. Stockwell; Rev. James P. Wilson, of Newark; Mrs. Henry L. Gregg; Matthew Wilson, the artist; Mrs. Dr. Wm. A. Brown; and N. H. Bishop, canoeist and author. The sharply-gabled cottage, on the higher open ground, is Montclaire Terrace.

STEAMBOATS.—The steamboat service on the lake is thorough, convenient, and satisfactory to the public generally. The "line" boats belong to the Lake Champlain Transportation Company, Capt. George Rushlow, General Agent, with office at Burlington, Vt. The boats on lake George and Lake Champlain (connected by train between the two) form a continuous day line through the two lakes. The Lake George boats are the "Horicon" and the "Ticonderoga."

The Horicon (side-wheel steamer), was built at the old landing near the outlet in 1876, re-built at Baldwin in 1890. It is of fine model, graceful poise, and can run 20 miles an hour under favorable conditions. The length of keel is 196 feet (203 over all), $8\frac{5}{10}$ feet hold, and $30\frac{7}{10}$ beam (about 52 feet wide over all). It is of 643 tons burden, and privileged to carry 1000 passengers. Three staterooms are provided for guests or passengers, and arrangements are made for dining such as desire it. The saloon occupies the entire breadth of the boat between the wheel-houses, and is 108 feet long, finished in butternut and black walnut and lighted with ground glass of two designs. Captain J. D. Reeves, commander.

The Horicon leaves Caldwell at about 9:30 A. M., on arrival of the train from the Hudson River night boats and touching at the various landings reaches

Baldwin about noon, where passengers are transferred by rail to the Champlain boat at Fort Ticonderoga, on which they may proceed northward, or may return south by rail via Whitehall. In the afternoon the Horicon returns from Baldwin connecting at Caldwell with train south to the night boats at Troy and Albany.

The Ticonderoga (side-wheel steamer), was built at the company's ship yard near the outlet, and launched August 23, 1883. Its dimensions are 172 feet in length over all, 28 feet beam and 9 feet hold. The greatest width at guards is 46 feet, ordinary draft when loaded 4½ feet. Its interior finish is of native woods and its general arrangement like that of the Horicon. Captain Richard Arbuckle, commander.

The Ticonderoga leaves Baldwin at 7:30 in the morning, touching at the principal landings and reaches Caldwell to connect with midday trains for the south. On arrival of trains from the south at about 4:30 P. M., the Ticonderoga returns to Baldwin, touching when required along the way. Fare either boat $1.50. Tickets are good for passage through the lake and return the same day without addition to the price.

The Island Queen, a small excursion steamer, trim and fast, built in 1890, makes morning and afternoon trips from Caldwell to Paradise Bay, landing at intermediate points. Fare 50 cents. Round trip one dollar. Captain, Everett Harrison; Pilot, Moses Finkle. This boat is 90 feet long, 18 feet beam, 4½ feet draft.

Small steamers may be chartered at from $15.00 to $25.00 per day.

ROADS AND DRIVES.—Not alone is Lake George to be enjoyed from the water. Its drives are many and delightful. Livery rigs, luxurious, stylish, and sensible, can be had here at Lake George, at reasonable prices, considering the stock which has to be carried through to accomodate the limited season. The finest are to be found at the stables of H. R. Levens & Co., at the Fort William Henry Hotel, and may be called by telephone from any house about the head of the lake.

The most picturesque road, and one in which the lake is the ever-present and ever-varying feature, is along the west shore to Bolton, which may be continued up past north-west bay and indefinitely among the mountains beyond. The undesirable feature is its sand, which makes the wheeling heavy a portion of the way, but not to such an extent as to be an unsurmountable objection. Lateral roads lead from this up the western hills and offer a variety of interesting if somewhat laborious ways.

The drive along the beach and down the east shore is an interesting one for those who enjoy woods and partially cultivated country. It passes by the ruins of Fort George Hotel, Crosbyside and a number of very pretty summer cottages and the Convent of the Paulist Fathers, " St. Mary's of the Lake " rising finally to the cleared space around the north side of French Mountain to overlook a great expanse of the lake. A branch road may be followed along shore to Lake George Park, on Dunman's Bay, notable as the summer place of Edward Eggleston.

The drive on the plank road to Warrensburgh, six miles north, where the Schroon River is crossed, is delightful, because of its shade. The ascent is gradual, rising through a picturesque notch between the mountains by the side of a babbling brook. The road bed is excellent for driving and usually as smooth and hard as an iron-like sand, quarried along the road, can make it.

The road to Prospect Mountain and the Mount Ferguson House on one of its summits seen prominently at the west, yields an interesting wood and field excursion and a grand prospect when the top is reached. There are two passable ways of reaching it, by the "old road," which is generally preferred, going by the way of the Warrenburgh road to the first toll-gate, thence west around the mountain, approaching the summit point finally from the southwest, by which the ascent is gradual, or by the "new road," which leads past the old Indian encampment and by a steep but shorter way arrives at the summit from the south. From the observatory here fully one-half of the lake can be seen, and the main peaks of the Adirondacks easily distinguishable by one who knows them by their outlies. Refreshments can be had here, and satisfactory accommodations for those who may wish to stop over night.

The most interesting drive, all things considered, of any at Lake George is the plank road south through French Mountain Pass, over the historic "Dark and Bloody Ground" to Glens Falls.

FORT GAGE stood on the hill that rises west of the road about one mile south and just beyond where the road from Fort George joins the plank road. The lines of earthworks may still be traced through the pines that now cover them. The slope was cleared of all timber down to the water's edge at the time of Abercrombie's advance in 1758.

BLOODY POND is a mile farther, at the left of the road and between it and the railroad. It is simply a stagnant pool that in the early part of the season is nearly covered with lily-pads and great white pond-lilies, and in the summer becomes almost dry. It is said that a party of the French (after driving the English into their fortified camp at Lake George, and being driven back in turn), were seated around the pond at sunset, was partaking of their evening meal, when they were surprised by a party of English advancing from Fort Edward, who poured in upon them a destructive fire. Totally routed, they fled in confusion, leaving their dead and wounded on the field. The dead were thrown into the pond by the English, their blood turning the water red, from which circumstance it received its name.

WILLIAMS' MONUMENT is about three miles south of the lake, and west of the plank road. It is a plain marble shaft, blue and white, standing on a huge bowlder, which is itself inclosed within an iron fence. It was erected in 1854 by the graduates of Williams' College, in memory of the founder of that institution. On it are inscriptions in Latin, to show the learning of those who erected it, and in English, telling what it is all about. From it we learn that it was "*Erected to the memory of* COLONEL EPHRAIM WILLIAMS, *a native of Newtown, Mass.*

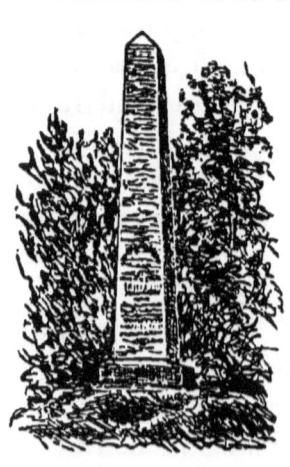

LAKE GEORGE.—J. D. WOODWARD.

who, after gallantly defending the frontier of his native State, served under General Johnson against the French and Indians, and nobly fell near this spot, in the bloody conflict of September 8, 1755, in the 42d year of his age.

The old military road ran along on the hill just above this spot, identical with the country road that is there now. A little way south of the monument, on this road, inclosed by an iron railing is a rude stone slab, supposed to mark the place where Col. Williams was buried. The stone bears the inscription

E. W.
1775.

COL. EPHRAIM WILLIAMS.

The drive continued south passes French Mountain, with its ancient and once celebrated Half-Way House, to Glens Falls, 10 miles from Lake George.

Glens Falls is the metropolis of Northern New York. It is the market and source of supplies of a large tract of rich, outlying country and of the northern Adirondack Wilderness. It is high and dry and delightful with shaded streets and a core of solid business blocks that rivals the city in appearance.

It has eight churches; a union free-school of splendid attainments; an academy, almost collegiate in its course; an opera house of fine appearance and appointments; numerous civic societies of varying objects; a military company (the 18th Separate) of high rank, a salvation army (small, but mighty of voice), electric street cars (running also to Ft. Edward and Sandy Hill), an excellent water system, uniformed police, electric lights, (arc and incandescent) with other modern necessities, and ten thousand inhabitants, who live mostly in houses of their own, and who are justly proud of the wide-awake town from which they hail.

The place was known to the Indians as "Che-pontuc," meaning a difficult place to get around. In 1762 a patent of Queensbury was granted to several of "our loving subjects" by George III, a large proportion of which patent was purchased by Abraham Wing, who erected a grist and saw-mill at the falls. Later, Wing sold his birthright for a mess of pottage—or to speak plainly—transferred his right and title to the name to a Col. Johannes Glenn for the price of a "wine supper" which the latter paid, and the name was changed to "Glenn's" Falls.

Of course you did not come to Lake George without something extra in your purse and Glens Falls will give you as fair an equivalent for that "extra" as any city in the country. Upwards of 50 stores—some of them models of elegance—supply the visitor with necessary or fancy articles unlimited, and those who may need anything, from an organ to an octopus, can usually have their wishes gratified here. To that end you are respectfully referred to the appendix, where almost every branch of trade and industry is represented by the cards of responsible firms.

If you would remain over night or for a dinner only, you may find hotels clean, wholesome and attractive. The Rockwell House, on Fountain Square, is the leading hotel and recognized as one of the best-kept houses in the State. It is very complete in all its appointments, provides an excellent table, and is thoroughly worthy of the very liberal patronage it receives. Rates $3 per day, $14 to $21 per week. C. L. Rockwell, proprietor.

The American Hotel, Monument Square is substantial and well ordered and enjoys a reputation for excellent fare and accommodations equaled by very few of the high priced houses of the country. Free bus to all trains. Rates, $2.00 per day. George Pardo, proprietor.

The Van Cott House is on South St. Rates, $2 per day. W. H. Van Cott, ex-County Clerk and good fellow generally, proprietor. The Granger house is near the fair ground. Rates, $1.00 per day. Wholesome and specially noted for its jolly pro-

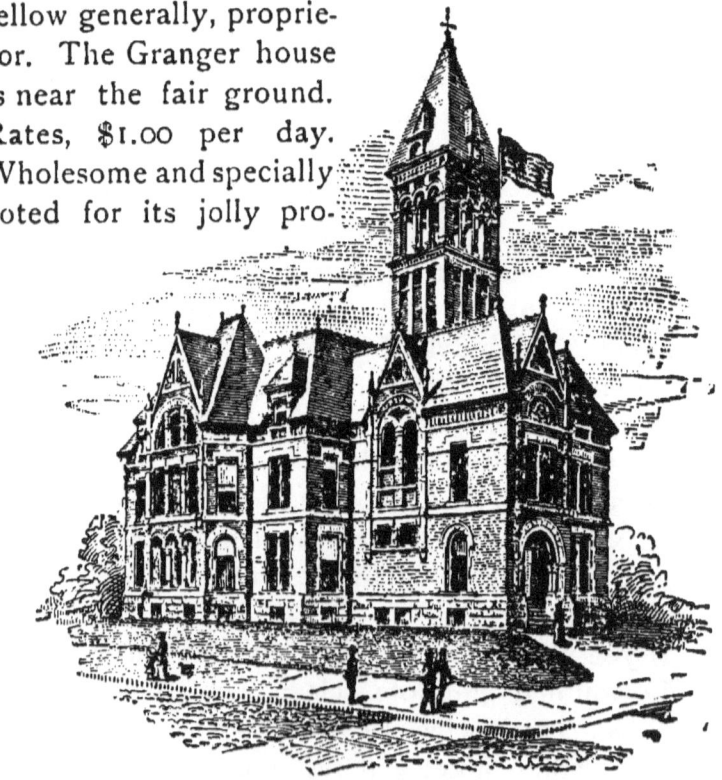

GLENS FALLS INSURANCE BUILDING.

prietor the one, only and original "Marcus." There are other hotels with a well established clientage and at reasonable prices.

The Glens Falls Insurance Company, located here, has through its agencies made the name of its birth-place familiar from Maine to Mexico. Organized in 1849, it has attained to national prominence and a reputation as one of the soundest institutions of the kind in existence. As a fact, many a Lake George tourist knows more about this company and its officers than about the beautiful village after which it was named. Its new building just completed on Monument Square is substantial, convenient and becoming as the headquarters of a prosperous institution that never failed in its obligations and never made a mistake. Such is its reputation and record. The officers of the company are J. L. Cunningham, president; R. A. Little, secretary.

Joseph Fowler & Co., gives employment to a large number of operatives. The factory on Glen St., between Monument and Fountain Squares is a very bee-hive of industry, well worth inspecting. Here are made all kinds of silk and flannel, satine and plain white shirts with collars and cuffs almost beyond number. The firm enjoys a reputation among dealers for producing high grade products with a superior finish, the pure soft mountain water with which it is supplied making perfect laundrying a possibility.

Van Wagner & Norris, in Opera House Block, make a specialty of fine custom work. Fine flannel and silk goods, neglige shirts and the countless necessaries of the well-dressed man, fully equipped for his summer outing can be had here. The firm is reliable, the work staunch and serviceable.

The "Canopy-top Buckboard," manufactured here, is celebrated from Maine to Mexico. The

"Time Globe," invented by L. P. Juvet, of this town, is known of scientific men in two hemispheres

The Glens Falls Terra-Cotta and Brick Co., a mile north of the village, employ upwards of 100 men in the manufacture of red and buff pressed and molded brick and architectural terra-cotta for exterior and interior ornamentation. They own extensive beds of marl and clay lying near, and a patent process for combining the same in a manner resulting in works of superior beauty and finish. J. M. Coolidge is president of the company, and Charles Scales superintendent.

Come with me down the Big Hill to the falls, You can see the mists that hang over the gulf and hear the sounds of its waters. Noisy mills now compass it about, and the rythmic sob of many saws mingle with its dull roar that never ends. A graceful new bridge erected by the Berlin Bridge Company, reaches out to the island from the north shore, while a stone arch spans the gulf at the south. At the south end of the long bridge, steps lead down to the flat rock, and near the lower end where it is notched and broken out, you may climb down to the level of the water, and enter the cave made memorable by Cooper in his "Last of the Mohicans."

In the dry season the volume of water is confined within the channels worn deep on either side, or finds its way in rivelets down across the pitted buttresses of black rock. Here the ledges, which in the spring freshets are covered with a foaming torrent, are worn smooth almost as polished marble. Na‘ural stairways lead in places to the top, and at intervals, holes in the rock, round and deep, are filled with water, with, possibly, at the bottom a remnant of the stone that under the action of the waters has worn itself away in vain turnings about in its deepening prison. One of these holes called the "Devil's Punch Bowl," is about six feet in diameter and the same in depth.

On either side are saw mills that have contributed to the town's prosperity, full of life and action at times, at others— and that too often —stilled by summer's drought or spring-time flood. On all sides are lumber piles. They line the banks of the river away above. They wall in the canal along up to where, at the "Feeder Dam," are more saw mills and more lumber piles It is estimated that the sawing capacity of these mills is 600,000 standard logs per annum. This means 120,000,000 feet of lumber, or 30,636$\frac{4}{10}$ miles of boards eight inches wide. If laid end to end they would extend around the earth with a long lap to spare, and in seven years lay a good plank walk to the moon, with no end of lath and slabs to throw at erratic asteroids or troublesome comets.

The lime business is next in importance to lumber. In quantity manufactured it is equalled in the United States only by Rockland, Me., and in point of quality stands at the head. The best rock yields, when calcined, from ninety-five to ninety-eight per cent. of the purest and whitest lime to be found on the continent. It is used extensively by tanners, bleachers of cotton goods and manufacturers of paper, wire, gas, glass, etc. The lime rock is embraced in an area of not more than 250 acres, beginning at the head of the falls, and extending in a narrow belt on either side for perhaps near a mile down the river, the strata dipping slightly toward the south, and disappearing under the hill along that side. For a depth of about thirty feet it lies in thin strata, then comes a stratum of grey marble, from two to three feet in thickness, and under this the solid black marble, twelve feet thick. This is almost a pure carbonate of lime; in its nativ estate of a bluish grey; calcined, it is whiter than snow. The tunnel on the south side from which the rock has been recently taken extends a considerable distance into the hill—a vast room with rock-roof, supported by many massive columns, and well worth a visit. Lime was first burned here about the year 1820, by Powell Shaw, then simply for home consumption. It was first manufactured and shipped to an outside market (Troy) by K. P. Cool, in 1832.

Lime Kilns—clouds by day and pillars of fire at night, are below the falls. They are of the patent or "perpetual" kind, with a burning capacity of 100 barrels each per day. Two sets of hands are required to attend to them, the fires running night and day. There are thirty of these lime-kilns. They are well worth visiting.

T. S. Coolidge is the general agent. Sub-agents are appointed in the various cities. About 500 men are employed in this industry. The average production for the past twenty years has been 450,000 barrels per annum, of which 200,000 are shipped annually to New York.

The black marble (which is the purest carbonate of lime in the world, with perhaps the exception of the Irish and Belgian marble), in its native state, is of a dark blue; wet, it becomes black; polished, it shines like jet. Blocks are quarried as large as four feet square and nine feet long. It is sawed into slabs for tiles, table tops, mantels, interior decorations and ornamental work. There are two mills here that saw the stone. See them saw and note how, under dripping water and sand, the toothless saws eat their way through the solid rock.

Wood pulp is manufactured in a large mill near the south end of the bridge, and vast quantities of wood that until recently, was considered almost valueless, now find its way in, in logs and comes out in thick sheets to be turned into paper in the adjoining mill.

The paper mill on the south side of the river has the perfected machinery of the day and reels off broad ribbons of paper a mile or more in length. The kind made is the kind used by the newspapers, and the fact that it is used by the Troy *Times*, the Brooklyn *Eagle* and the New York *Sun* proves its remarkable political flexibility.

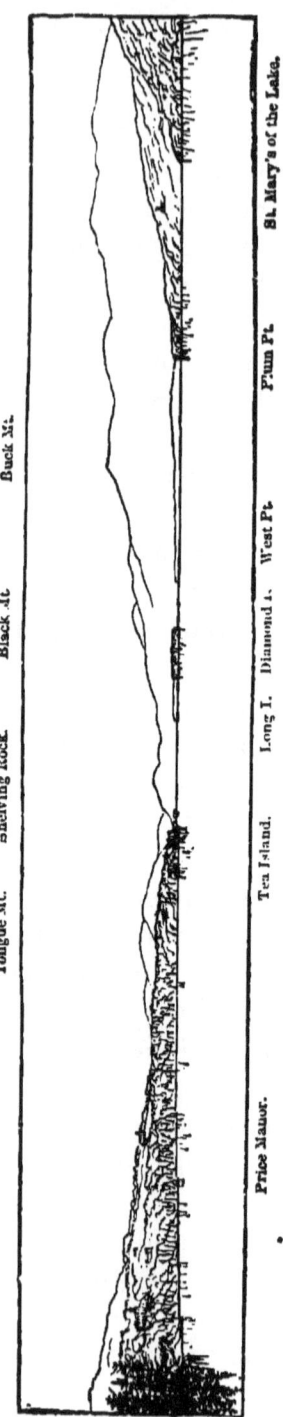

LAKE GEORGE.

DOWN THE LAKE.

NOTE.—By aid of accompanying large map, and the outline cuts distributed through the book, the reader should have no difficulty in locating all points of interest seen from the steamboats. Travelers from the north should read paragraphs as numbered in reverse order, beginning at Ticonderoga. "East" and "west" indicate side to look from the channel usually taken by the steamboat. Distances given are air-line distances from Caldwell, unless stated differently.

1. From the south. The outreaching point from the west terminates in Tea Island, about a mile distant (see outline cut); over this is Tongue Mountain; a little at the right, the round top of Shelving Rock; about two miles beyond Tea Island, at the right, is Diamond Island; beyond this, partially hidden by it, is Long Island; at its right edge is West Point. About two miles away, on the right, is Plum Point; on the high ground, a little nearer, the summer place of the Paulist Fathers. Still nearer, among the trees, is Crosbyside. Over the beach, at the east, is the Fort George Hotel; and back toward the south, the ruins of the old fort. Toward the west is Prospect Mountain, and at its base along the west shore, is the village of Caldwell, known to the postal department as Lake George.

2. TEA ISLAND (west) is a little gem of an island, somewhat resembling the crater of an extinct volcano, with the rim broken away on the east side, forming a beautiful harbor in miniature.

Tradition says Abercrombie buried gold and valuables here; and a goodly share of the surface has been dug over, at different times, by the treasure seeker—some one suggested that the digging was for fish-worms, but the idea is too absurd to be entertained for a moment.

The handsome building on the west side, one mile from the depot, is the residence of W. J. Price, of New York. A. D. F. Randolph, poet and publisher, has a modest cottage among the trees west of Tea Island. Rev. Dr. Butler, of Philadelphia, is near by. Rev. Dr. Tuttle occupies a cottage near the shore, north of Tea Island. Price Manor, residence of the late Col. W. W. Price, is on high land, two miles from the depot. The octagon building, at the waters edge, is *not* a light-house.

3. ST. MARY'S OF THE LAKE (east), a mile north of Crosbyside, in a grove of young trees, is the summer place of the Paulist Fathers. This society is composed of priests, whose work is chiefly that of missionaries, something akin to that of the old Jesuits. Their convent is in New York, presided over by its founder, the Rev. Father Hecker. The Paulists also own Harbor Island, and camp there a portion of the year.

4. PLUM POINT (east), a half-mile north of convent, received its name, it is said, because of the large quantity of plums raised here. The casual observer will see no plums, and may not see the point of this. (Mild joke.)

5. DUNHAM'S BAY opens up on the right. At its head is Lake George Park. Edward Eggleston

the stalwart author, lecturer, and divine, has a cottage here.

6. DIAMOND ISLAND (west), near the centre of the lake and three miles from its head, was so named because of the quartz crystals found upon its surface. It was fortified and used as a military depot by Burgoyne, after his capture of Ticonderoga in 1777, and the same year was the scene of an engagement between the forces then in possession (the English) and a party of Americans under Col. John Brown, which resulted in the defeat of the latter. In 1820 it was occupied by a family who gained a living by the sale of crystals found there. East of it are two nameless little pyramids of broken rocks. which go to make up the 220 islands of the lake.

7. CRAMER'S POINT (west, 2¾ miles from Caldwell). It is said that this was an island, when the islands all belonged to the state; but a former owner of the adjoining shore looked upon it with longing eyes; and one night the kind waves, or something equally efficacious, filled up the intervening space with earth; the island and the shore clasped hands across the muddy chasm; the twain were made one flesh, and no law was found to put them asunder. At the west is the tasteful villa of George H. Cramer, of Troy.

8. THE ANTLERS (west 3½), Jerome Burton, proprietor. Capacity 100. Rates $2 per day; $8 to $12 per week. P. O., Hill View. House completed and opened for 1891.

9. REID'S ROCK is just north of Cannon Point (west, 3¾ miles). A man named Reid, whose love for rum had taken him across the lake one stormy night in late autumn, was found on this rock, in the morning, frozen stiff, and covered with ice from the dashing spray.

10. ORCUT BAY is entered between Reid's Rock and Cannon Point. "The Healing Spring" is just over the ridge, west of this bay, and may be reached along shore from Caldwell. The visitor should see this spring, and talk with its honest, odd owner, "Uncle Joe," as he is universally called, who has firm faith in the efficacy of the water to cure all the ills that flesh is heir to.

11. DIAMOND POINT (west 4 miles) comes next The quartz here, like that of Diamond Island, occasionally yields very pretty crystals. Sampson Paul, an Indian, who flourished over half a century ago, once killed a panther with a common fishing-spear, here, as the poor brute was coming out of the water benumbed with cold.

12. DIAMOND POINT HOUSE (west, 4½ miles). John Coolidge, proprietor. Capacity, about 50. Large boats do not land. Reached by wagon from Caldwell, or by small steamers. P. O., Hill View.

13. CANOE ISLANDS (west, 4½ miles), east of Diamond Point House, about midway between it and Long Island. Here the American Canoe Association was organized in 1880. The islands are owned by N. H. Bishop, and others.

14. LONG ISLAND is the largest island at Lake George, being something more than a mile in length. The deed by which it was transferred by King George to private parties, bears date of July 4, 1770. The house near its centre is the summer place of its owner, Dr. D. S. Sanford, of New York.

15. ASSEMBLY POINT (right, 4½ miles from Caldwell), known for years as West Point, has been rechristened with a new name as above. The Lake George Assembly, organized in 1888, is an association owning or controlling about 100 acres of land here. The resident trustee is Dr. D. S. Sanford, and its establishment is due almost entirely to the exertions of that tireless worker, who sums up the objects and aims of the community in a nut-shell, as follows:

"Its plan is three-fold,—Recreation, Reason, Religion. Its scope is to blend these three R's. While we are recreatingly rusticating we may also reason reasonably and reveal religion in the everyday life. It will attain its end by encouraging everything that is manly, noble and healthful in sport, by interesting lectures from interesting men every Tuesday, Thursday and Saturday at 4 o'clock, free (never more than an hour in length), and through Sunday services (11 A. M. and 4 P. M.), by eminent divines, stimulate the desire to live a nobler, better and purer life. A number of tents have been provided for rental at reasonable figures. Parties furnishing their own tenting outfits may camp within the grounds at 10 cents per day—children, God bless them! nothing. A store and restaurant is on the ground—no extortions permitted. Lots are for sale to approved purchasers only, subject to such rules and regulations and restrictions as will best conserve the comfort, happiness and convenience of congenial families that we hope to gather in a homelike colony here, where Mrs. Grundy and other fashionable follies have small part, and where Mrs. Ostentation and Mrs. Extravagance are altogether absent. If you are law-abiding, order-loving and Sabbath-respecting, be one of us. If you are not, don't."

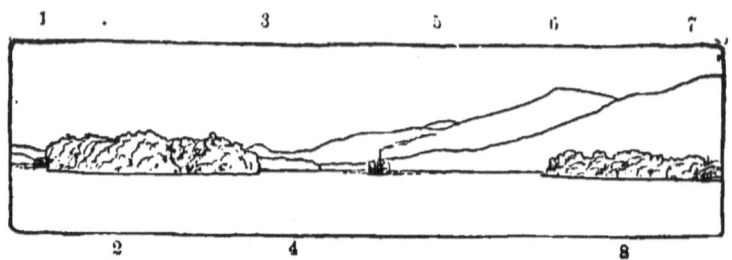

VIEW NORTH FROM NEAR DIAMOND ISLAND.

Dome Island; 2 South Island ; 3 Shelving Rock Mountain ; 4 Long Island , 5 Black Mountain ; 6 Buck Mountain ; 7 Pilot Mountain ; 8 Assembly Point.

"The Brooklyn," William M. Frommell, proprietor, is at Assembly Point. Rates on application.

16. HORICON LODGE (right, 5½ miles by steamer), George A. Ferris, manager. Capacity 100. $2.00 per day ; $8 to $12 per week. P. O., Cleverdale.

17. SHELDON HOUSE (right, 6 miles). Attractive grounds. Capacity, 80. Rates not given.

18. EAST LAKE GEORGE HOUSE, Franklin Gates, proprietor. Landing, Sheldon's Point. Capacity, 60. Rates, $1.50 per day : $7 to $10.00 per week. P. O., Kattskill Bay.

19. GROVE HOTEL (right, 7 miles), E. Wetmore, proprietor. Capacity 75. $2.00 per day ; $8.00 to $10.00 per week. P. O., Kattskill Bay. Land at Trout Pavilion. Boat or carriage in attendance on arrival of steamer from south.

20. TROUT PAVILION (right, 7 miles), John Cronkhite, proprietor. Capacity 100. Rates, $2 per day ; $9 to $12 per week. P. O. address, Kattskill Bay. The accommodations offered are in three buildings, the two nearest the lake connected at one corner by their piazzas, which extend on three sides. One building contains parlor, dining-room, &c., the others, private parlors and sleeping rooms. In the inner angle formed by the two, is an open, tree-shaded floor for dancing. Bowling and outdoor sports have been provided for. The accommodations are good, the table clean, wholesome and abundant. An attractive feature is the boats and the attention given to the legitimate sport of fishing. Open June to October. A pretty steam yacht, the "Latona" is here subject to charter at $15.00 per day, $10 for a half day.

21. The Albion is north of the trout Pavilion. Rosa Phelps, proprietor. Capacity 40. Rates $2.00 per day, $10.00 to $12.00 per week. Mayflower Cottage, still further north, is a private boarding house, capacity, 30.

22. KATTSKILL HOUSE is on the high terraced bank at the north dock, shaded by a thrifty grove of birches. Capacity about 100 guests. Rates, $2.00 per day; $10.00 to $12.00 per week. Open from June 15th to October. A. P. Scoville, proprietor. The post-office (Kattskill Bay) is located here and a wire connecting with the Western Union telegraph is in the office. Good fare is furnished and an excellent patronage held here.

23. ELIZABETH ISLAND appears as a point of the shore north of the Kattskill House. The Manhattan Club, composed of graduates of New York College, make it their summer camp ground.

24. PILOT MOUNTAIN (right, 7 miles, air line from Caldwell), is nearly sharp at its summit, descends steeply to the lake at points where we lately

MARION HOUSE.

touched, and further away, at the south, slopes gently down to the fertile vale of Harrisena.

25. BUCK MOUNTAIN (right, 9 miles) is a grand rocky, round-featured mountain, along the east, rising 2,000 feet above the lake. It is sparsely wooded at the summit. This, with Pilot Mountain on the south, is locally known as the deer pasture. Phelps' Point is at the lake, a little south of the highest part of Buck Mountain. A passable road leads out along shore to the Kattskill House.

26. MARION HOUSE (west side, 5¾ miles from Caldwell), D. W. Sherman, proprietor; H. L. Sherman, manager. Capacity 400. Rates, $3.50 per day; $14 to $25 per week.

Recent additions have made this one of the largest houses at the lake. It has been remodeled from office to attic. Its public rooms are spacious, delightfully open to the air, richly furnished throughout, and contain many unconventional appliances that tend to enjoyable ease. It is lighted with gas throughout, and heated by steam. Its sleeping rooms are large, furnished modestly but with excellent material, and supplied with superior beds. An elevator renders all floors almost equally convenient and leaves little choice in rooms, unless there are preferences in points of compass. Electric bells communicate between guests' rooms and the office, and a wire from the office connects with the Western Union Telegraph. The sanitary conditions are pronounced perfect. Soft, sweet water is brought to the house through pipes, from a spring on the west mountain. All steamboats from north and south land at the dock. A feature of the table supplies is the butter and milk, from a herd of Jerseys belonging to the Marion farm.

The grounds surrounding the Marion are extensive and attractive. It has the advantage of approach by land, as the picturesque road from Caldwell runs along the shore, past the house. Back of the house are rugged bluffs, and forests almost as wild as they were a hundred years ago. The views of the lake are broad and far-reaching. Livery rigs of standard excellence can be had at established prices. A feature here not common to the Lake George hotels is the tally-ho coach, " Marion," on which, a moonlight dash along shore with a select party, or a trip over the mountains, represents the acme of rare coaching experience, and more fun than an old-fashioned trip across the continent. The Marion is an exceptionally attractive place.

The Agawam which stood on the shore of the bay a half mile north of the Marion was destroyed by fire in 1890.

27. VICTORIA LODGE (East, $7\frac{1}{2}$ M.), John W. Harris, proprietor. Address at Kattskill Bay, for particulars.

28. DOME ISLAND (East, 9 miles), near the centre of the lake, next claims our attention as being the highest of Lake George's 220. Seen from the north and south, it has the appearance of a huge emerald dome, somewhat flattened, but bearing enough of the appearance to justify the name. This island was purchased from the State in 1856, for $100.

29. RECLUSE ISLAND (west), is just west of Dome, our course taking us between the two. Pliny T. Sexton of Palmyra, owner. This island was the subject of the earthquake hoax of 1868, when it was reported in the New York papers as being sunk 80 feet below the surface. A graceful bridge connects it with what was once known as Sloop Island. Belvoir Island is west of Recluse Island, and is the property of Rev. Geo. W. Clow, of White Plains.

30. LAKE VIEW HOUSE, R. J. Brown, proprietor. Capacity, 100. Rates, $3 per day; $12 to $15 per week. P. O., Bolton.

This house has earned for itself that unfailing sign of approval—the repeated return of old guests to familiar rooms and places, their number augmented annually by new friends and kindred spirits. The view is unsurpassed for quiet beauty, as revealed in retreating headland, pretty grouping of island forms and the lovely gate-like openings of the distant Narrows, with giant Black Mountain beyond.

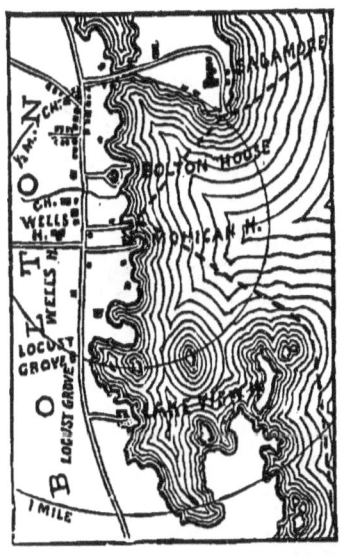

Mr. Brown makes a very pleasant landlord, agreeable and obliging. The grounds around the Lake View are pleasant, and the effort has been quite successfully made of leaving nature's perfect work untouched while relieving it of unsightly objects, and making all parts trim and accessible. There are detached buildings here for bowling and billiards, open space for croquet and tennis, retired walks, cozy seats and pleasant outlooks. A pleasant addition is the detached building back among the trees con-

LAKE VIEW HOUSE.

taining a large room for general assembly, hops, etc. A "dark room" on the grounds is a convenience that is appreciated by amateur photographers. A steam catamaran, built under Mr. Brown's direction plys between the house and Bolton Landing, about a mile distant, transferring guests of the house and baggage free.

South of Lake View House is Concordia Bay, so names from the fact that its shores have been a favorite camping ground of the Union College boys. The attractive cottage on the point beyond, overlooking the lake from its rocky perch and appropriately called "Buena Vista" was built in 1889 by Robert C. Alexander of the New York bar. He is the owner of the tract which forms the entire west shore of Huddle Bay, and extends back to the highway running from Caldwell to Bolton. Extensive improvements have recently been made on this property in clearing up, opening drives and vistas, and laying out the lake frontage into cottage sites. On one of these, northward from Buena Vista, Rev. J. D. Kennedy of Brooklyn, is building a handsome cottage, which will be ready for occupancy during the present season. Charles Dudley Warner is on record as saying this is one of the most exquisite spots on Lake George.

32. LOCUST GROVE is back at the northwest of the Lake View House. Capacity 75. Rates, $2.00 per day, $9.00 to $15.00 per week. George R. Fish, proprietor.

The handsome villa back of the bay indenting the shore north of the Lake View, with statues distributed about the ample lawn, is the summer place of William B. Bement, of Philadelphia.

LAKE GEORGE.

33. MOHICAN HOUSE, E. B. Winslow, proprietor. Capacity 100. Rates, $3.50 per day, $12.00 to $20.00 per week. Free transfer of guests and baggage to steamboat. Open the year round. P. O., Bolton. This is one of the desirable houses of Lake George and has been noted for years as the resort of people of culture and refinement. There is no ostentatious display but on the contrary it seems to 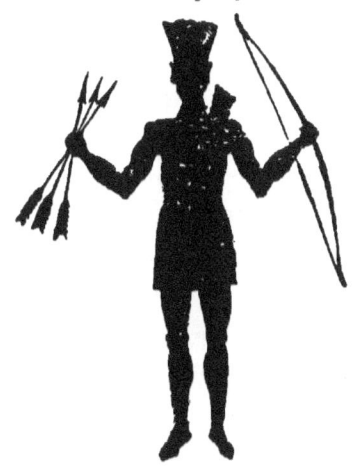 withdraw from the public gaze and seclude itself among the trees and flowers that deck the lake front. The lawn is shaded by locusts and maples, and the long point protected by an expensive sea-wall terminating at the substantial dock where the little steamers land—a favorite place with guests who can here catch delicious whiffs of the faintest breath that may be stirring across the lake. This was once the main landing for Bolton, with the "line boat" coming and going, but the runners and guests from other houses, and travelers passing over the grounds, made it too public a thoroughfare for those who here sought quiet and rest, and a public dock was built in the bay at the north that might accommodate all the hotels of that section.

The house is a long, low, rambling structure after the southern style, with piazzas facing the lake and extending along its south side. The trees press their heavy tops against it, effectually shading it from the too ardent rays of the sun, but underneath the wind can pass freely and the views of the lake are interfered with scarcely at all. The parlor and dining room afford space for general assembly and there are neat, cozy sleeping rooms, nicely furnished with choice of ground or second floor. Such as may want greater seclusion than the main building affords can find spacious and desirable quarters in the cottage on the shore of the lake at the north, while toward the west is a newer and larger building with superior furnishings and equipment.

The table and service is excellent—neat, clean and appetizing, and in its dainty niceness very attractive to the refined taste, and yet the lusty ones with natural appetites sharpened by boating excursions or in tramps among the picturesque hills, find an abundance that should satisfy the most ravenous.

For amusement, croquet grounds are laid out under the trees, while lovers of tennis or polo, or the national game, find space on the level grounds at the west. The roads of Bolton are varied and picturesque, and those who enjoy riding or driving can secure means for the pleasure here. For boating or fishing, a fleet of lake boats dancing on the water south of the point invites attention, and guides and fishermen stand ready for service. Here also is one of the finest bathing beaches on the lake with sandy bottom sloping gradually out into deep water, and roomy bath-houses fitted with every convenience.

From the tribe of Uncas came the name, and on the tall flag-staff that stood out on the point for many years stood a wooden warrior defying sun and storm, and his silhouette as it was reared against the bright sky is to-day the totem of the modern "Mohican."

The legends of the place are many. One is of a beautiful Indian girl who was brought a prisoner from the shores of the Great North Lakes by the Mohicans in one of their periodical war raids through " The Lake that is the Gate of the Country." Arrived at their village here, a young chief, the pride of the nation, gazed into the stranger's dark eyes and was made captive by her grace and beauty. He would have taken her to his wigwam in preference to any maiden of his own tribe but the old women of the nation had chosen for him another bride, and when he again went on the war-path, and the cruel old men and women only were in possession of the camp, it was decreed that the daughter of the northern tribe should die. They bound her to the stake, piled faggots high around her slight form and the fire was lighted, but as the crackling flames curled upward, a supernatural figure that shone like a blazing comet—stronger than a buffalo and swift as the wind—swept through the circle, scattered the blazing brands like playthings right and left, and seizing the willing captive, dashed out again before the awe-struck crowd had recovered from their terror. Running through the growing corn to the middle of the field at the west he sprang to the top of a large stone, and from it flew upward with his burden, over the hills, and the girl was never seen more. Curiously enough also the young brave came not back with his party. He had vanished out of their life. But thereafter, at every coming of the tasseled corn, some warrior of the tribe was slain by a mysterious being who came out from dark Oulusca—" The Place of Shadows " west of the great peaks—a warrior who shone like the fox-fire of the lowlands and whose cunning and might were beyond the power of human brave. The body of his victim was always found lying across the stone from which the stranger sprang over the hills, and the blood-stains on it took the shape of picture-writing where the people read their fate; for the Great Spirit had decreed that for every fire-touched hair of the maiden's head a Mohican brave must die, until the tribe should be no more.

As proof, the rock still lies in the field west of the house, and the old gardener, Franz Richter, points out the footprints of the mysterious fire-chief, the blood-stains of the victims that were afterward offered up; of Indian faces and forms; of animals and birds and flowers and growing trees. See Franz and hear the story from his lips of the "Sacrificial Stone" of the Mohicans.

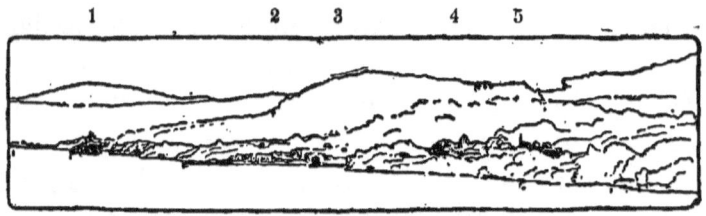

BOLTON BAY FROM THE NORTHEAST.
1 Lake View House; 2 Mohican House; 3 Steamboat Dock; 4 Bolton House; 5 Church of St. Sacrament.

North of Mohican Point is the old "line" boat landing. North of this the pretty cottage occupied during the season by James Palmenter, the Cranberry King, of Chicago. Toward the northwest on a rocky bluff is the church of St. Sacrament (Episcopalian), its bell in front in a small tower by itself.

35. BOLTON LANDING is 9½ miles north of Caldwell. The line boats land regularly here to receive and deliver mail.

LAKE GEORGE. 49

The Bolton House, standing back a little way from the landing, will accommodate 100. Rates, $3 per day; $10 to $15 per week. John Vandenbergh proprietor. West of the landing is the Roman Catholic Church. A Baptist Church is at the hamlet of Bolton Landing, a quarter-mile further north. Here also are the Stewart and Goodman houses—places of good repute and moderate prices. Back of the ornate balustrade along shore north is Ganouskie Cottage, belonging to Ezra Benedict, of New York. The large, red-roofed house with glass summer-house attached north of the Pine grove is occupied by R. W. Wilson, local manager for Commodore Simpson. Then comes a red structure with tall, round tower, belonging to E. B. Warren, and occupied by his fisherman "Alex" Taylor.

36. **Hotel Fenmore** is at the west end of the long bridge that connects Green Island with the main land. Capacity 20. The red building on the heights beyond belongs to Mrs. Putnam. Farther north is the summer residence of George W. Silcox.

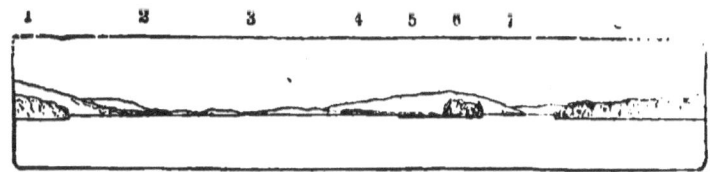

SOUTH FROM THE SAGAMORE DOCK.

1 Dome Island; 2 Elizabeth Island; 3 Kattskill Bay; 4 Long Island; 5 French Mountain; 6 Recluse Island; 7 Canoe Islands; 8 Belvoir Island

The Sagamore (on Green Island, west, 9½ miles), M. O. Brown, proprietor. Price of Board, $3.50 to $4.00 per day; $17.50 to $25.00 per week, according to time and season. Open June 20th to October. The hotel stands among the trees at the south end of the island, flanked by handsome, modern cottages. The style is that popularly supposed to belong to the sixteenth century. The cluster which may be considered the hotel proper is built at varying levels, delightfully uncertain of number, picturesque and pleasing, connected by open corridors with charming outlooks; its varied porticoes, balconies and gables admirably displayed in colors that harmonize well with their native surroundings. Its interior finish is plain, but rich and substantial, showing massive beams, fireplaces of artistic designs in terra cotta, tinted walls and joiner

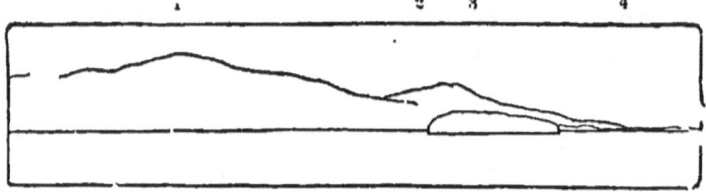

SOUTH EAST FROM SAGAMORE DOCK.

1 Black Mountain. 2 Pilot Mountain: 3 Dome Island. 4 Katskill Bay

work in native woods. The main hall and office and the principal parlors are on the main floor, looking out upon a velvety lawn with flower bordered walks sloping under the trees and revealing delightful vistas of lake and islands beyond. The line steamers land on every regular trip through the lake, connecting with the trains at each end. The accommodations and general management of the Sagamore are of the best.

Of the attractive cottages along shore on either side the one nearest the dock on the west, "Bellevue," is occupied by Gen. Robert Lenox Banks of Albany.

The next, "Nirvana," is the summer place of J. B. Simpson, Jr., of New York, vice-commodore of the Lake George Yacht Club. East, and nearest the dock is the cottage of George Burnham, and beyond it the turreted "Vapanak" belonging to E. B. Warren—each a study architecturally and all charmingly picturesque.

From the Sagamore dock, the boat runs almost due east toward the entrance to the Narrows, about two miles distant.

38. CROWN ISLAND (west, 10 miles), owned by G. M. Dilly, of Palistine, Texas, and for sale, is a short distance beyond the Sagamore landing. North

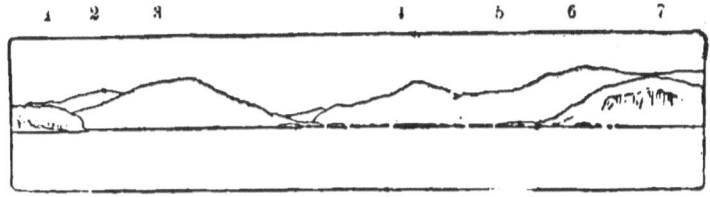

THE NARROWS FROM THE SAGAMORE DOCK.
1 Cr wn Isl nd ; 2 Northwest Bay ; 3 Tongue Mou t i ; 4 Black Mountain ; 5 Fourteen Mile Island ; 6 Mt. Erebus ; 7 Shelving Rock Mountain.

West Bay (or "Ganouskie" as the Indians called it) extends northward about four miles beyond Crown Island.

39. OAHU ISLAND (west, 11 miles), is the property of Gen. P. F. Bellinger, of Elizabeth, N. J. Gen. Bellinger occupies the cottage toward the south, while the one near the north end is the summer place of J. W. Moore, Chief Engineer U. S. Navy.

40. TONGUE MOUNTAIN rises rugged and broken, west of the Narrows, and, sloping gradually southward, terminates in Montcalm Point, owned by Mr. J. Buchanan Henry. West of the mountain is

Northwest Bay. "Green Oaks," the summer place of E. Corning Smith, of Albany, is on Turtle Island, lying northeast of Montcalm Point.

41. THE KENESAW (East, 11 miles from Caldwell), is on Fourteen Mile Island, H. H. Van Aranam, proprietor. Capacity 100. Rates, $2.50 per day; $10 to $15 per week. The house, without

THE KENESAW

making any pretentions to architectural beauty, is cozy, convenient and comfortable. Its piazzas and numerous summer houses scattered about the island are attractive and suggestive of good times.

Why called Fourteen Mile Island the oldest inhabitant does not pretend to say. It is presumed however, that fourteen miles was the estimated distance from Fort William Henry, before actual measurement demonstrated it to be less. The island has an area of twelve acres, portions of which are extremely picturesque in combination of rock and soil, and with fine specimens of oak, chestnut and Norway pine. Its shores are rocky and broken in some places, in others rounding smoothly over into the deep water, with huge, lichen-covered boulders, smooth, rocky floors carpeted with thick mosses, and hollows filled with waving ferns. Its varied features have made it a favorite resort with artists, who here found fitting studies for every variety of mood.

On the east, separating it from the mainland, is a narrow and deep channel, through which the largest steamers can pass. Here is another dock where excursion steamers land.

HEN AND CHICKENS at the south is a pretty group of islands, on one of which Delavan Bloodgood, surgeon U. S. N., has built picturesquely after the fashion of an East Indian bungalow.

Following along the rocky shore south of Fourteen Mile Island you find many pretty bays and headlands. At one point a little brook makes out over a beach. If you will enter the sandy gate you find yourself within one of the most charming thicket-guarded bays on the lake. Alighting where a noisy brook tumbles in, at its head, and following up a little way, you will be rewarded by the sight of a perfect little gem, called Shelving Rock Falls.

42. THE HUNDRED ISLAND HOUSE (right, 11¼ miles from Caldwell), R. G. Bradley & Co., proprietors. Capacity 100, Rates, $2.50 and $ 3 per day ; $10 to $17.50 per week. P. O., Shelving Rock. Picturesque, and with pictures on every side, this section is a favorite among artists, the lovely grouping of the islands and the grand lines of the surrounding mountains affording beautiful studies from this point. *En passant,* the house has a convenient dark

THE NARROWS—J. D. WOODWARD.

THE HUNDRED ISLAND HOUSE. 53

room, fitted up for the accommodation of those who "press the button" whether they "do all the rest" or leave it for others to do.

The location is capital for a summer house, affording a protected harbor for small boats, a new dock easy of approach for large. It is built in the most substantial manner possible, and with a degree of finish seldom applied to hotels designed simply for summer occupancy. The table is exceptionally wholesome, and served in an attractive manner.

HUNDRED ISLAND HOUSE.

Fresh milk and vegetables come from the farm belonging to the house. The post-office — "Shelving Rock" — is in the hotel office, and the telegraph is close by.

A stairway leads up to the sightly observatory, from which the roof may be gained, and a view obtained that has hardly its equal anywhere on the lake, showing the broad, open water toward the south and west, the hundred islands of the Narrows, and the lake stretching away to Sabbath Day Point at the north.

THE PEARL POINT HOUSE is one of the leading hotels of the Lake. Its furniture and appointments are liberal and complete in all respects. Rambling, quaint and profusely ornate in architectural design, the buildings attract much attention and admiration. Nestling amid abundant shade trees, surrounded by piazzas, with tasteful, elaborate and admirably kept grounds, little imagination is required to invest the place with unusual interest. Including two handsome cottage buildings, or dormitories, the establishment affords accommodations for one hundred and fifty guests. From its opening, in 1876, it has been exceedingly well managed, and has secured a permanent reputation and patronage of superior character. It is conducted on strict temperance principles, and on that account has peculiar attractions to many.

The location in the Narrows, faced and flanked by "The Hundred Islands," on account of the shelter afforded by the islands, make boating delightful in any state of the wind, while the fishing of the neighborhood is excelled nowhere on the Lake. That both may be enjoyed without stint, the proprietor makes a special feature of his boat livery, having provided a numerous and really elegant fleet of boats of various styles and sizes, suitable for every requirement, all equipped with the best in the way of oars, cushions, etc. Telegraph wires and daily mails enable guests to communicate readily with the outer world. D. W. Sherman, proprietor. Rates $3.50 per day, $12.00 to $21.00 per week.

THE NARROWS.

Ranger Island is west of Pearl Point. The pretty cottage with sharp peaked tower belongs to a devoted disciple of old Isaac Walton, Justice F. E. Ranger, of Glens Falls. Next at the north is Juanita Island, where the Bullard Brothers — and sisters — come every summer. The "Glen Club" — composed of some of the solid men of Glens Falls, and commonly called the cold water club, for obvious reasons — become boys again every year on the island north of Juanita.

Phantom Island is next, with its attractive cottage and tastefully decorated summer houses and grounds. It is owned and occupied during the summer by Hon. Jerome Lapham, of Glens Falls. It was formerly the home of "the hermit," J. Henry Hill, who came here in 1870, built the house and occupied it alone until 1876, when he was adjudged insane, and removed temporarily to an asylum, where he soon recovered. He belonged to a family of artists, and was himself one of considerable ability — his professed object here being the study of nature.

Gem Island and cottage, northeast from Phantom, is where another solid Glens Falls club "receives," during the season. Gravelly Island is the nearest large island toward the north from Pearl Point.

Over under the west shore is Turtle and Phelps' Islands. Camp Colvin, on the latter, belongs to a Glens Falls man — in fact Glensvillians have pre-empted a considerable portion of this attractive group of islands, and still cry for more.

LAKE GEORGE.

BURNT ISLAND is the largest of the Hundred Island group, and occupies a central position toward the north. On it half wild goats have for several years lived and bred.

AS-YOU-WERE ISLAND is the last of the group near the west shore.

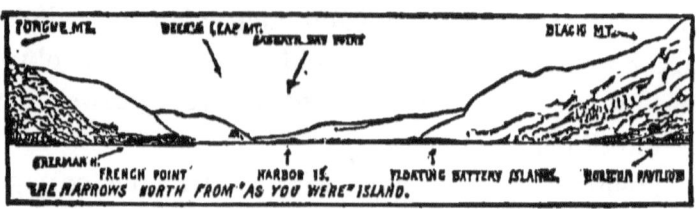

LITTLE HARBOR ISLAND, east of the last named has on its north border one of the curious holes in the rock supposed by some to have been the work of the aborigines.

FORK ISLAND, its shape suggesting the name, terminates the cluster at the northeast.

PARADISE POINT, a beautiful peninsula—site of a proposed hotel colony—extends from the east shore, separating Red Rock Bay on the south from Paradise Bay on the north, the latter guarded by a cluster of very pretty islands.

There are others, a multitude of them, some rising abruptly from the depths, moss-draped and thicket-crowned, while others only see the light when the water sinks to its lowest level. All around are treacherous shoals and reefs, and when the light is right and the water rough, you may see the surface checked and spotted by the bright green that marks their position, while the little steamer, with many a graceful turn, threads the labyrinth as the verdant gateways open and close along her course.

FRENCH POINT projects from the west shore, 13 miles north of Caldwell. The shore here is rugged and broken, running in places straight up from the water, Tongue mountain rising sheer from the little plateau. The Sherman House that stood here was burnt to the ground at the close of the season of 1889.

BLACK MOUNTAIN stands on our right, the monarch of the lake stretching away to the north, seeming to recede as we approach and travel with us, its granite crest lifted over two thousand feet above us, its rocky sides seamed and scarred and reddened by fires that have swept over it in times past. A sentinel, it seems, overlooking the whole lake and mountains round about; the first to welcome the rising sun, and at evening, glowing in the splendor of the dying day, while the valleys below are misty with the shadows of coming night. From its summit, 2,661 feet above tide, and 2,315 above Lake George, nearly the entire lake may be seen. To the north is Lake Champlain; at the east lie the Green Mountains; on the west and north the Adirondacks rise one above another, while away toward the south, like a thread of silver, stretches the mighty Hudson. Don't forget to take an extra blanket or heavy shawl if you make the ascent,—and don't forget the luncheon. Horicon Pavilion, which stood on the cleared space southwest of Black Mountain called Black Mountain Point, was destroyed by fire April 21st, 1889. It was a poem in wood and stone, a work of art that seemed here a part of nature's self. From this point an excellent road ascends to the top of Black Mountain.

Tongue Mt.   Deer's Leap   Black Mountain   Mt. Erebus

NORTH FROM FOURTEEN MILE ISLAND.

Ship I.   Badger's I.   French Pt.   Uncas I.   Glen I.   Phantom I.   Gravelly I.   Pearl Pt.   100 Island H

THE NARROWS.

HALF WAY ISLE is under the west shore, the centre of a circle, of which the circumference is the rim of a mountain that rises, amphitheater-like, around its western side. As its name indicates, it marks the centre of the lake.

THE "THREE SIRENS," lovely and inviting, but surrounded by dangerous shoals and reefs, are out in the middle of the lake nearly opposite Halfway Island.

HATCHET ISLAND is one of the same chain; the derivation of the name is unknown, but tradition connects it with a good little boy who couldn't tell a lie.

ONE TREE ISLAND it is just outside the channel. The stump is all that remains of that "one tree."

FLOATING BATTERY is north of One Tree Island, the southernmost large island of a group lying along the east shore, opposite the highest point of Black Mountain. In the little bay on its south margin is the remains of what is said to be one of the two "castles," floating batteries, or gunboats, built to accompany Abercrombie down the lake in his advance on Ticonderoga, in 1758. The name is sometimes applied to the entire group, as it stretches along shore.

MOTHER BUNCH is the name given to the northernmost member of the group, because, it is said, of a fancied resemblance between a portion of the island and an old woman; it is a beautiful tribute to the memory of the old lady any way, while the classic elegance and appropriateness of the name only fell short of absolute inspiration in that it was not advanced a step farther to "Grandmother" Bunch, and done with it.

The CIVES ROCK is a solid wall, breaking off perpendicularly from the mountain slope on the right, north of Mother Bunch; water constantly drips over its face, and cives, a species of garlic growing in tufts, and liked as a relish by some, spring spontaneously from its fissures; the largest boat can be laid up along side of this rock in still weather. A venerable landmark, known to have been there sixty-five years, is an old stub, projecting a little above the surface, and swaying about just outside the usual course of the steamer; below the portion that has been worn down by the ice it is four feet in diameter, its point downward, and supposed to be anchored in the bottom of the lake. The water here is seventy feet in depth.

THE HARBOR ISLANDS are near the center of the lake, the west channel passing close by their western border; they are owned by the Paulists, who received a title to them from the State, in 1872, and who occupy them occasionally as a camping place. The group is the first of any considerable size on the west side, north of the Narrows, and was once the scene of one of the bloodiest engagements in the history of the lake. On the 25th of July, 1757, a party of between three and four hundred English, commanded by Col. John Parker, left Fort William Henry, and under cover of the darkness proceeded down the lake on a scout. When near this place, at dawn of the next morning, dark objects shot out from among the islands and the surrounding gloom to meet them, while the savage war-whoop sounded on all sides. As the yelling horde advanced the English became panic-stricken and sought safety in flight. But their clumsy barges were no match for the light canoes of the enemy. Some threw themselves into the lake and succeeded in reaching the shore, there to be pursued and struck down by the savages.

One hundred and thirty-one of the English were killed outright, twelve escaped, and the rest were taken prisoners. Of the latter, Father Roubaud, a Jesuit priest, says in his "Relations": "The first object which presented itself to my eyes on arriving there was a large fire, while the wooden spits fixed in the earth gave signs of a feast—indeed, there was one taking place. But oh, Heaven, what a feast! The remains of the body of an Englishman were there, the skin stripped off and more than one-half of the flesh gone. A moment after I perceived these inhuman beings eat, with famishing avidity, of this human flesh; I saw them taking up this detestable broth in large spoons, and, apparently, without being able to satisfy themselves with it; they informed me that they had prepared themselves for this feast by drinking from skulls filled with human blood, while their smeared faces and stained lips gave evidence of the truth of the story." The good father attempted to reason with them, but to no avail. One said to him: "*You have French taste; I have Indian; this food is good for me,*" offering at the same time a piece of the human flesh to the horrified priest.

LAKE GEORGE.

"CAPTAIN SAM"

Vicar's Island is just north of the Harbor Islands Here, on its northern border, an affecting incident transpired once, of which Captain Sam Patchen, who lived at Sabbath Day Point at the time, was the hero. One winter's day he conceived the idea of sailing his grist to Bolton mill on the ice. So, piling the bags of grain into the old cutter, with a pitchfork, held firmly in his hands, for a rudder, he hoisted sail and sped away before a strong north wind.

The ice was "glare," and the cutter sailed well — remarkably well; but there was not so much certainty about the satisfactory behavior of the steering apparatus. The old man, it is said, was given to spiritual things occasionally, and had, on this occasion, evidently hoisted in rather too much rye in the liquid form to conduce to the safe transportation of that in the bags. The craft insisted on heading directly for the island, and could not be diverted from its course—it was of the kind called "jumper"—a mettlesome old jumper at that, and the captain had a great deal of confidence in its ability to do whatever it undertook. So he decided to jump the island. He tried it. It was not, strictly speaking, a success. The cutter reached the shore, and paused against a rock, but Sam was anxious to get along, and continued on with the bags and finally brought up in a snow-drift.

Captain Sam was *always* dignified, and on this occasion it is said his manner of resting on that snow-drift was remarkably impressive. Even the snow felt moved, and the island itself was touched, and when he came out and set his radiant face homeward he was *not* a Sam of joy or a Sam of thanksgiving, but a Sam abounding in language that would set a mule driver up in business, and bring despair to the boss canvasman of any circus traveling.

Deer's Leap Mountain is on the west, a little way north of Vicar's Island. The top is rounded, the side facing the lake a perpendicular wall of rock. at its foot are great fragments of rock that have fallen from time to time, and said to be a favorite resort for the rattlesnake. Once on a time a buck pursued by hunters, was driven to the brow of the precipice, a pack of yelling hounds close at his heels.

"Not the least obeisance made he;
Not a minute stopped or stayed he—

but leaping fearlessly, far out over the giddy height, was impaled on the sharp point of a tree below.

HULETT'S LANDING (east, 18 miles from Caldwell), Henry W. Buckell, manager. Capacity, 125. Rates, $2.50 per day; $9 to $14.00 per week. Open June to November. P. O., Hulett's Landing.

The surroundings are exceedingly wild and interesting. The plan for the entertainment of guests is of a central building containing the general office, with post and telegraph offices, a second containing assembly, and music rooms; a third with the dining-room, kitchen, etc., connected with the first by a picturesque covered walk, and several detached cottages that may be rented by families or assigned to guests in common with the rooms in the main building. Steamers land going each way. It can be reached also *via* Chubb's Dock on the D. & H. R. R., 5 miles east. A wagon road has been made from this point to within a mile of the top of Black Mountain.

MEADOW POINT is north of Hulett's on the same shore. A cluster of pretty cottages here, fitted up with neccessary conveniences may be rented with or without board. Here Cyrus Butler hoped to establish a summer school of music, painting and botany but in his death the enterprise lost its inspiration and "Horicon" an ardent admirer. He was one of the most lovable of men, a sympathic friend and a generous enthusiast whose benefactions were limited only by his means as many a struggling genius can mournfully attest.

HOG'S BACK is the rugged mountain back of Meadow Point. Near its highest point Putnam and Rogers once came upon an Indian encampment, and, after the heroic manner of warfare in those days, left none to tell the tale. Illustrative of the brutal nature of the man and the spirit of retaliation which to some seemed to justify the most cruel measures, Rogers, it is said, killed an Indian baby by dashing its brains out against a tree, and when remonstrated with by Putnam said, "It's a nit and will be a louse if I let it."

The red-roofed, Swiss-like building, on a point beyond Meadow Point, is the summer place of De Lorm Knowlton, of New York. North of Hog's Back stretches Spruce Mountain—strikingly bold and precipitous.

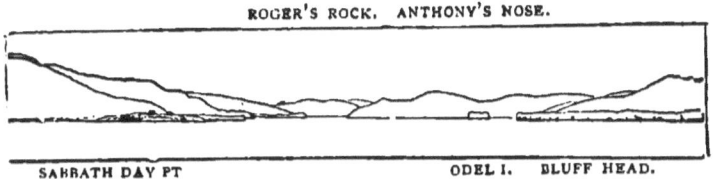

BLUFF HEAD is the long point extending out from the east shore. The late Rev. A. D. Gillette, D. D., for many years pastor of Calvary Church, New York, made this his summer home. His widow and sons, Dr. Walter R. and David G. Gillette have cottages here now.

From Hulett's Landing, we run diagonally across the lake to Sabbath Day Point, about two miles dis-

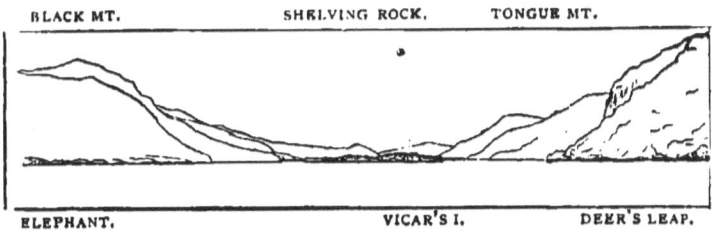

tant. As we draw near to the dock glance backward toward Black Mountain. Note how the old giant asserts his supremacy, rising up and o'er topping his less stately supporters. A little further along and he is again the stately centre of the picture

THE ELEPHANT stands back there at the north end of Black Mountain. See his well-formed head toward the west; his eye, and the rift that marks the outline of his massive jaw; the wrinkled neck and great round back, with scattered bristles of dead pines clearly defined against the sky beyond.

SUGAR LOAF MOUNTAIN is over at the left of the Elephant. Its summit, viewed from a little distance north of Sabbath Day Point, looks very like a pig lying down, with his sharp nose pointing east. These animals were, undoubtedly, a part of the lot created "in the beginning."

TWIN MOUNTAINS are seen in the southwest from Sabbath Day Point. The southernmost one is the Deer's Leap, the other locally known as Bloomer Mountain.

SABBATH DAY POINT (west, about 19½ miles from Caldwell). Capacity, 25. P. O., Sabbath Day Point. F. A. Carney, Proprietor.

Sabbath Day Point has been the scene of many stirring incidents in the history of Lake George. It commands the approach by water on either hand, and would naturally be selected for a camping place by parties who had reason to expect an enemy near. Here, in 1756, a body of provincials, under Putnam and Rogers, repulsed a superior force of French and Indians; and on the 5th of July, 1758, Abercrombie, with his splendidly equipped army of over fifteen thousand men, landed for rest and refreshment, remaining until near midnight, when he moved down the lake, leaving immense fires burning, to give his watchful enemy the impression that he was still there.

In September of the following year Gen. Amherst, with twelve thousand men, drew his boats up on the sandy beach west of the house, and passed the Sabbath with appropriate religious ceremonies. To this circumstance is sometimes ascribed the name, although it had been called Sabbath Day Point for some years before. It is said also, but on doubtful authority, that an engagement occurred here in 1776 between fifty Americans and a force of tories and Indians, resulting in the defeat of the latter.

In 1765, eleven years before the engagement spoken of, we find record of a house here, occupied by one Samuel Adams. In 1798, Capt. Sam Patchen (hero of the cutter ride to Vicar's Island) built a log-house near the site of the present building, since which the Point has never been without its resident family, The late owner of the Point, also named Sam—Capt. Sam Westurn, lived here for many years, a genial pleasant companion. The place is very homelike, wholesome and pleasant.

The Indian Kettles, at the edge of the water on the bay north of the Point, are good specimens of rock boring—but you wonder whence the grinding power that should create them—by the side of quiet water.

GRACE MEMORIAL CHAPEL was erected here in 1885 in memory of the wife of Mr. Norman Dodge, daughter of Rev. A. D. Gillette, D.D. It cost

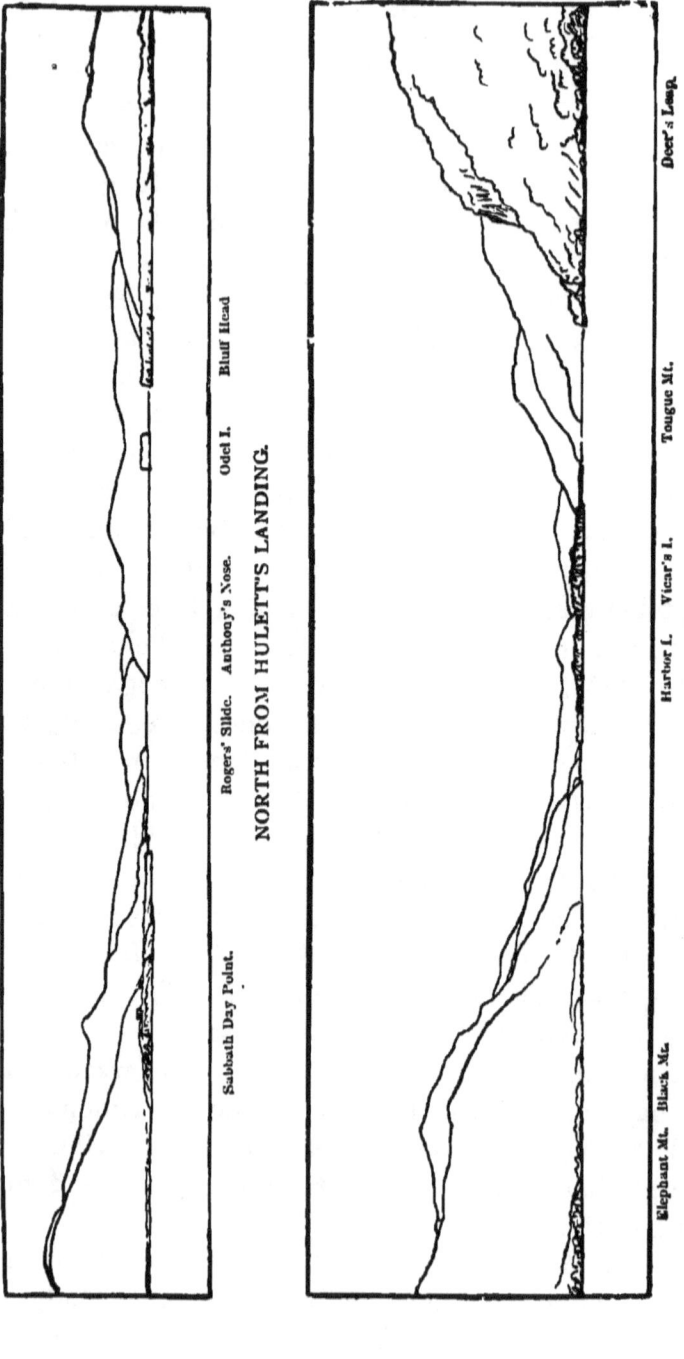

about $7,000, contributed by the New York families who had made this place their summer home.

On the west shore south of Sabbath Day Point are summer cottages severally owned in the order here given, by J. M. Jackson, J. J. Wilson, W. H. Van Cott and Rev. A. H. McKinney. On the point north of the steamboat landing is the summer place of J. F. Chamberlain Esq., of New York. A mile further north are the cottages of Rev. C. F. Hageman, Rev. D. B. Wyckoff and Dr. Landon.

SILVER BAY (landing, telegraph and post office, west 22 miles from Caldwell) J. J. Wilson, proprietor. Capacity, 75. Rates $10 to $15 according to room. The house is a little distance back from the lake to which the land slopes easily, looking, with its surrounding buildings like a little village. It has its own post office called "Silver Bay" in common with the charming harbor near by. It is supplied with the necessary conveniences insuring comfort and furnishes admirable quarters and fare. Boating, bathing and fishing facilities are ample for all the acquatic needs and pleasures of guests. For hunting and climbing among the western hills—which stretch so invitingly along parallel with the lake and up which, back of the house run paths like network over the open space—nature has presumably supplied all that may be considered necessary, or if not it takes but little time here in the gloriously bracing air of Lake George, to get the requisite energy and strength, and the exhilaration of the climb and the beautiful views to be had when on its summit, or the game found in its depths, well repays one for the exertion.

SCOTCH BONNET, four miles north of Sabbath Day Point, is a flat rock, lying west of the channel, and but a little above the surface. It was so called because of the resemblance which a cedar tree, that once grew on its surface, bore to a Scotch cap or

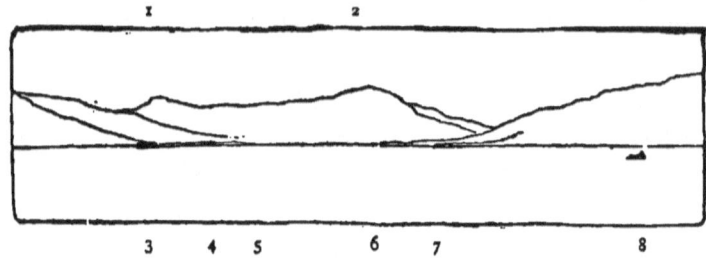

SOUTH FROM NEAR HAGUE.
1 Sugarloaf Mt.; 2 Black Mt.; 3 Odel Is.; 4 Bluff Head; 5 Hulett's Landing; 6 Sabbath Day Point; 7 Slim Pt.; 8 Scotch Bonnet.

"bonnet." The "Umbrella Tree" stands on the point near by, beyond which as the steamer rounds into the western bay is seen Hague with its picturesque village stretching along shore.

HAGUE.

HAGUE is situated on a broad, sweeping bay, at the west side of the lake, 28 miles from its head. The general character of its scenery is peaceful, lacking the grandeur of the Narrows, but here the artist will find plenty of matter for study in the great variety of foliage, lichens and mosses, the many-colored rocks, the rugged islands and the graceful elms, whose slender branches droop and sway like the weeping willow, the like of which is seen nowhere else at the lake.

Good bass fishing is found near by, and two fine trout brooks render the place attractive to those who throw the fly, while the shore, all the way back to Sabbath Day Point, is considered good hunting ground. A walk up the valley road, north of the house, gives a number of the most charming bits of scenery imaginable.

THE PHŒNIX HOTEL is the large, white three-story building seen a little way north of the steamboat landing. The house will accommodate fifty, comfortably. A level, grassy lawn stretches from the house out to the sandy beach along the water front. Rates not given. George F. Marshall, proprietor.

"THE HILLSIDE," John McClanathan, proprietor, is situated a few rods north of the Phœnix. Capacity 75. Rates, $1.50 per day; $8 to $10 per week. Open June 15 to October.

TROUT HOUSE, Charles H. Wheeler, proprietor. Capacity 40. Rates, $1.25 per day; $7 to $8 per week. Open all the year. Here the most wholesome of country fare is provided, and homelike comfort rules the establishment from one year's end to the next. It is one of the places where you are made to feel that your welcome is not always gauged by the length of your purse. "Charley" can tell to a nicety just where the big trout is to be

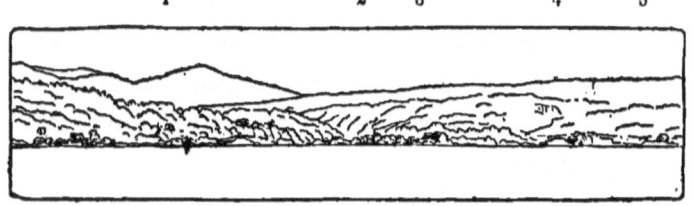

HAGUE FROM THE SOUTHEAST.

1 Steamboat Landing; 2 Phœnix Hotel; 3 Hillside House; 4 Trout House; 5 Rising House.

found, and, next to landing it himself, he enjoys showing some favored one the way to do it. A tennis court is a pleasant feature here.

THE RISING HOUSE a short distance north of the Trout House, on the flank of a hill that, rising into quite a mountain toward the west, comes thickly wooded down almost to the door. It commands a most extensive view and is well spoken of for its table and general accommodations. Will accommodate about 25 guests. B. A. Rising, proprietor.

ISLAND HARBOR (west, 1 mile north of Hague landing), A. C. Clifton, proprietor. Capacity 50. Rates $1.50 per day, $8 per week.

Island Harbor is the name given to the cluster of houses on the west shore of the bay, formed by the enclosing group known as Cook's Islands. It is much frequented by sportsmen, and has a record for big fish, approached by few places along the lake. The location, while retiring, shows lovely vistas through the islands, and affords safe boating, even in the roughest weather. The table is excellent.

Free conveyance between all houses and the steamboats.

WALTONIAN ISLE is the outermost and largest of the group of nine outside Island Harbor. The steamboat rounds close to its rugged shores.

Ten miles away at the south, the "Elephant" stretches his huge bulk across the lake; over his head Black Mountain stands guard, growing misty along the distant narrows.

Near by, at the north, is Friend's Point, a pleasant, tree-bordered meadow, quiet and beautiful enough now, but of old, the scene of bloody engagements, being then, as now, a favorite camping ground.

On the right is Blair's Bay, setting well back into the eastern shore. At its head are cleared fields in the town of Putnam—a bit of civilization reaching out from the section beyond, and seeming almost foreign in its lack of interest to the rest of Lake George.

ANTHONY'S NOSE extends west along the north side of Blair's Bay. It is heavily wooded, excepting in spots where a cliff is presented or where its western point rounds over sharply into the lake. From a position well back on the south side of Blair's Bay can be seen a perfect face in profile, with smooth brow, Roman nose, firm lip and bearded chin, looking out toward the west from the perpendicular wall at the second mountain step. It cannot be seen from the passing steamer.

ANTHONY'S NOSE.

We pass close to the point of the mountain, so near that a stone could be easily tossed against its iron-stained sides, and we struggle with incipient profanity to note where some vandal quack has paraded his nostrums before a long suffering publc, desecrating the face of nature, aye, even outraging its very nose with his vinegary compound, and, with the wish father to the thought, we look down into the depths to see if, perchance, retribution did not overtake him in the act and leave some record for our gratification.

This is said to be the deepest portion of the lake, put down as being anywhere from four to five hundred feet in depth, and a stone loosened from its bed above, is heard in dull, heavy thuds as it leaps from crag to crag down through the water to the unseen bottom.

ROGERS' SLIDE is toward the west, a mountain nearly a thousand feet high, with smoothly rounded top and precipitous sides. It is rich in minerals, many beautiful specimens of garnet having been found along its summit, and also graphite or black lead, which exists in considerable quantities. Nearly half of its entire height is a smooth wall of rock descending at a sharp angle to the water's edge. It is said to have received its name from the following circumstance: In the winter of 1757-8, Robert Rogers, with a small party of Rangers, was sent to make observations at Ticonderoga and Crown Point, where he fell in with a party of the enemy, and the skirmish which ensued resulted in the total defeat of the English. Rogers escaped, and, pursued by the savages, made for the summit of what was then called Bald Mountain, probably, with the object of putting in practice the ruse which his dare-devil nature had suggested. Arrived at the brow of the precipice, he threw his "luggage" down the steep walls, and, *reversing himself* on his snow-shoes, made his way down through a ravine, at the southwest, to the lake; thence around to the foot of the slide. The savages, following to the edge of the mountain, where the track of the snow-shoes seemed lost in the path made by a falling body, expecting, of course, that whoever had attempted it could not have reached the bottom alive, must have been considerably surprised to see the brave major making off on the ice toward the head of the lake. It is probable that they took it for granted that he had actually gone down the steep wall; this admitted, signs that at another time would have lead to the discovery of the ruse at once, were overlooked, and they, feeling that he must be under the protection of the "Great Spirit," with characteristic reverence for their Deity, desisted from further pursuit.

ROGERS' ROCK MOUNTAIN may be ascended by a good path leading from the hotel north of the slide to the top, from which point may be had a view of surprising grandeur and extent. On its summit, looking like a tiny bird cage from below, is seen a summer house built by Boston's celebrated divine, the Rev. Joseph Cook, whose birth-place is just over the other side in pleasant Trout Brook Valley. Mr. Cook spends much of his summerings at the old homestead and may often be seen on the mountain-top, looming grandly against the sunset sky.

The ROGERS' ROCK HOTEL stands on a bold promontory just north of Rogers' Slide, and supplies the long felt need of a first-class house at this end of the lake. Around it cluster some of the most interesting reminiscences of the past; near by are deep waters and running brooks; from its commanding position it looks out over the narrowing waters of the outlet and south to where Black Mountain stands guard over the way ; backwards, a road winds through the wood and up the mountain, and woodland paths run here and there with guide boards pointing the way to interesting places. The steamboats land on the regular trips. Small boats in variety give facilities for fishing or pleasure excursions. A cottage on the height, nearly 150 feet above the house, and another at the lake shore, give guests a choice in altitudes afforded by no other hotel at Lake George. The house abounds in quaint, old-fashioned furniture and bric-a-brac. An immense fireplace gives genial warmth to parlor and connecting office. Soft mountain spring water, never failing in the dryest times, supplies the house and is carried to every floor, Post-office created for the house named "Rogers Rock" and telegraph office are here. Capacity 125. Rates, $3 per day; $17.50 to $28 per week. Hon. T. J. Treadway, manager.

BALDWIN, 32 miles from Caldwell, is at the end of steamboat ride, and here cars are taken for the Champlain steamers at Fort Ticonderoga landing.

ROGERS' ROCK FROM BALDWIN

HOWE'S LANDING is the bit of circling beach north of the dock. Here Abercrombie, with his army of 15,000 men, and Lord Howe, their life and moving spirit, landed on the 6th of July, 1758, and advanced toward Ticonderoga.

The French, who retreated as the English advanced, burned their bridges across the outlet, thus compelling their enemies to follow along the outer circle made by the stream as it sweeps around toward the east and south where it empties into Lake Champlain. In the valley, north of where we cross the outlet, Howe, at the head of his detachment, fell in with a portion of the retreating French, and a skirmish ensued. At the first fire the gallant young leader fell, and with him the hopes of the army. Abercrombie sounded the recall and did not advance again until the evening of the next day; this delay allowing the French to strengthen their defences at the old lines, and is probably the main reason for the defeat of the English at that place.

PRISONER'S ISLE is out in the lake east of Howe's Landing. Tradition says the French used it as a prison pen. Another version of the account places the English in possession, and a party of French—taken by Abercrombie in the earlier stages of his advance on Ticonderoga, and who escaped during the night by wading ashore—their guests, and properly enough receives marked attention on account of this very interesting story. It seems characteristic, however, of the head that controlled the whole movement, and suggests the thought that, if this eminently sagacious and far-seeing warrior, Abercrombie, trusted to the depth of the water to keep a drove of Frenchmen, like a drove of sheep, he did not immediately, on discovering that they actually intended to fight, surrender himself and army to them; but, no! by the most profound strategy he succeeded in making a brilliant retreat, and escaped with the remnant of his army — consisting, then, of only about thirteen thousand men — from Montcalm's overwhelming force of thirty-five hundred!

Toward the north, the lake rapidly narrows down to a mere creek, hastening to its fall, and the crystal water is discolored by the clay of the bottom. Formerly the boats ran nearly a mile further to the old dock.

Here at the outlet, once when May flowers were blooming in the wood, came the martyr priest who gave it the beautiful name of St. Sacrament, and was the first white man to gaze upon its beauties. A century passed, and, in 1757, another Frenchman went southward over its waters; the first came with bible and cross preaching peace; the second with fire and sword and a hord of savage beasts to fated Fort William Henry.

The following year came Abercrombie, to be driven back while the flower of the British army lay on the bloody field of Ticonderoga, and the next year, slow but resistless in its march, came the army of Amherst, and before it, the French were swept northward, their hold on "the lake, that is the gate of the country," gone forever.

MOUNT DEFIANCE, a little elevation east of the outlet, which can hardly be dignified by the name of mountain, commands old Fort Ticonderoga, ly-

ing over on the other side, and received its name when, in 1777, Burgoyne, from its summit, trained guns on the old fort.

The UPPER FALLS of Ticonderoga may be seen on the left as we approach to cross the outlet. It is one of the best water privileges in the country, supplied by a reservoir that never floods or fails. A cotton factory, pulp mills, etc., here, give employment to a large number of operatives.

TICONDEROGA (village), three miles from Baldwin and two from Lake Champlain, contains about

1,500 inhabitants. The water-power is considerable, and the stream navigable for small steamers from the foot of the lower falls out into Lake Champlain.

THE BURLEIGH HOUSE is at Ticonderoga village. E. J. Wood, proprietor. Rates, $2.50 per day; $10 to $20 per week. It was named after Hon. H. G. Burleigh, of national fame, who owns the building. It is the leading hotel of this section, and offers many attractions to summer visitors. It is a handsome building, with modern conveniences, including electric bells, electric lights, and steam heat. It spreads a superior table. It is nearest to Fort Ticonderoga of any house that the visitor, will ordinarily, care to patronize, and it is a convenient centre for various interesting drives. Next to having back the good old times when staging was the regular means of crossing from one Lake to the other, is an excursion over the historic ground, in the tally-ho belonging to the Burleigh House, with the accompanying oratorical historico-legendry accompaniment, by the driver, which will be furnished if due notice be sent in advance, to the proprietor of the Burleigh House, at Ticonderoga.

FORT TICONDEROGA (lake station) is at the east foot of Mt. Defiance, five miles from Baldwin. Here Lake George trains connect with the Champlain steamers and cars from the north and south. The old fort can be seen at the north, about a mile distant from the landing. Refreshments can be had at the old Ft. Ticonderoga Hotel by the lake shore.

Tickets are good, either by boat or rail, as far north as Plattsburgh, giving travelers the choice between an afternoon spent on the lake, or at the Ruins. At Plattsburgh, passengers by boat and train unite.

LAKE CHAMPLAIN.

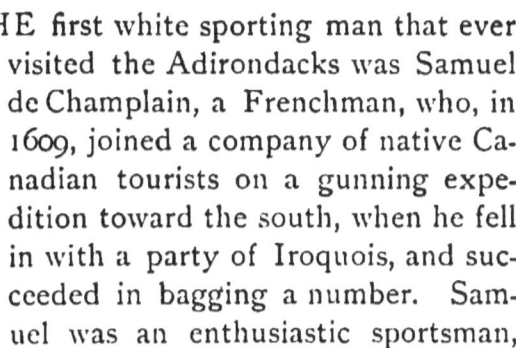

THE first white sporting man that ever visited the Adirondacks was Samuel de Champlain, a Frenchman, who, in 1609, joined a company of native Canadian tourists on a gunning expedition toward the south, when he fell in with a party of Iroquois, and succeeded in bagging a number. Samuel was an enthusiastic sportsman, and of a vivacious, happy disposition, as witness his felicitous description of the manner in which he, at the first shot, brought down three out of four Aborigines, who broke cover, then pursued and killed some others. After this adventure, which happened the same year that Hendrick Hudson sailed up the river that now bears his name, and 11 years before the Pilgrims landed on Plymouth Rock, he wrote an account of the affair, modestly calling the sheet of water explored after himself — Lake Champlain. Just two centuries after his passage in a canoe, the first steamboat was launched on the lake. When Champlain came, the Indians called the lake *Cani adere quarante*, spelled in various ways, and said by learned authorities, who copy it from some one else, to mean "the lake that is the gate of the country." By the early French, who did not choose to recognize Champlain's right to the name,

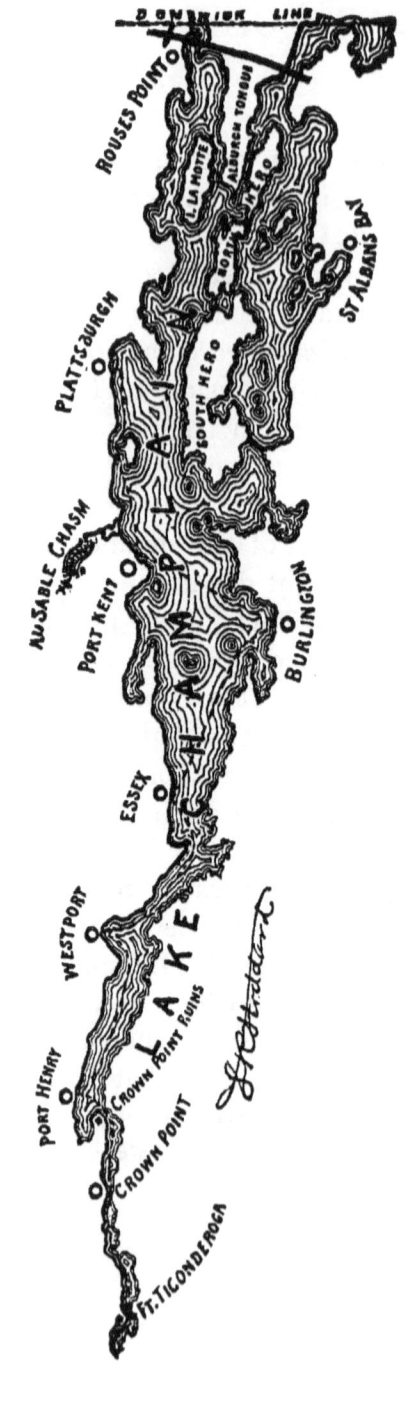

it was known as *Mere les Iroquois*, or "Iracosia." A book published in 1659 speaks of it as "the lake of Troquois, which, together with a river of the same name, running into the river of Canada, is 60 or 70 leagues in length. In the lake are four fair islands, which are low and full of goodly woods and meadows, having store of game for hunting. Stagges, Fallow Dear, Elks, Roe Bucks, Beavers, and other sorts of beasts." In shape it is very like a long, slim radish, with Whitehall at the little end.

On the east is Vermont, sweeping away in a broad, cultivated plain, that gradually ascends to the ridges of the Green Mountains. Along the southern and central part of the lake, the rocky western shores step down to the water's edge and backward, rise peak on peak, wild, broken, and grand — the Adirondack Mountains. Here and there are bits of cultivated land, and breaks in the mountain-gateways to the wilderness. Then, as you go north, the mountains fall away back into the interior, and a level, well-cultivated country presents itself.

Its length, from Whitehall to Fort Montgomery, is $107\frac{1}{4}$ miles; its greatest width, which is near the outlet of Au Sable River, is $12\frac{1}{8}$ miles, and greatest depth (at a point $1\frac{7}{8}$ miles southeast of Essex Landing), 399 feet. Measuring down into Missisquoi bay, the extreme length of the lake may be found at about 118 miles. Its elevation above tide is 99 feet. It contains a number of beautiful islands, principally near the north end, the two largest known respectively as North and South Hero, and collectively as Grand Isle, a county of Vermont.

WHITEHALL.

THE D. & H. R. R., extending along the west shore of the lake, in an air line, between New York and Montreal, is the main artery of travel between the two great cities. At various points, rail or stage routes diverge, leading to the central portions of the wilderness.

2. WHITEHALL* is at the head of Lake Champlain; 219 miles north of New York, 78 from Albany. It was originally called Skeenesborough, after Col. Philip Skeene, who accompanied Abercrombie in 1758; was wounded in his attack on Ticonderoga, and, after Amherst's victorious advance the following year, was appointed commandant at Crown Point, at which time he projected the settlement. In 1765, he obtained a grant of the township, and, in 1770, took up his residence here. On the breaking out of the Revolution he took sides with the Royalists, accompanied Burgoyne in his expedition against Ticonderoga, and was captured with him at Saratoga. His property was confiscated by act of Legislature in 1779.

At Whitehall, the train from the south divides,—a part going east, the remainder north, along the principal street, through the tunnel, and across the marsh-bottomed basin, toward a notch cut out of its farther rim. Just before entering the rock cut alluded to, we see on the east a short double crook, in a narrow channel, known as "Fiddler's Elbow," where, under water, are the hulks of some of the vessels engaged in the battle of Plattsburgh in 1814. On the high point of rocks just over and slightly to the north of the Elbow is Fort Putnam, where Gen-

---

* In going south along Lake Champlain, read numbered paragraphs in reverse order, begining at Rouse's Point, page 153.

eral Israel Putnam lay in ambush, waiting for the French and Indians under the command of Marin.

The train skims over the surface of the marsh on the long trestle, straight as an arrow flies, for a mile, and over the draw at the outlet of South Bay around which Dieskau led his men to attack Fort Edward, in September of 1755.

Winding in and out, we continue along the west shore. On the east, at intervals, are the odd, little numbered light-houses, and posts where lanterns are hung nights to mark the tortuous channel. Low, reedy islands and points float outward from the shores, and the grand, rocky gateways, opening up as we advance, reveal vistas of wondrous beauty, of far-reaching water, and of the blue of distant mountains.

Twenty-three miles north of Whitehall is the steamboat landing, and the junction of the branch road from Lake George with the main line running north.

THE STEAMER VERMONT, Captain B. I. Holt, commander, belongs to the Champlain Transportation Co. It was built in 1871, rebuilt and refurnished in 1892. It is 271 feet long, 36 foot beam, 65 foot beam over all. It runs regularly between Plattsburgh and Ticonderoga, leaving Plattsburgh at 7 A. M., touching at Bluff Point, Port Kent and Burlington, arriving at this point about noon. Returning, leaves on arrival of passengers from Lake George and the south. Passengers by the morning boat through Lake George will find the Vermont awaiting them here. Dinner is served on board. And, by the way, the dinners served on the steamer Vermont have been noted for years for their wholesomeness, and for the plethora of good things with which the table is loaded. On the other hand, the appetite which a ride over Lake George or Lake Champlain gives a body is also a constant source of wonderment—and it costs just a dollar here to do justice to the one and satisfy the other.

3. THE RUINS OF FORT TICONDEROGA can be seen on the promontory lying about one mile north of the steamboat landing. Here were enacted the principal events in the play of the lake; here savage and civilized tribes contended for the country on either hand; here two great nations struggled for the prize of a continent which neither could retain, and precious blood fllowed like water for this, the key to the "gate of the country," by its position elected to become historic ground.

Claimed by the Hurons and Algonquins on the north, and by the Five Nations on the south, Lake Champlain was permanently occupied by neither. It lay between two sections that were continually at war with each other—the bloody middle ground, over which each party in its turn swept, carrying ruin in its path. This had made the lovely shores a solitude. Thus Champlain found it when, in July, 1609, he sailed south with the Indians from the St. Lawrence to make war upon their southern enemies, and "encountered a war party of the Iroquois on the 29th of the month, about ten o'clock at night, at the point of a cape which puts out into the lake on the west side." In the morning a battle ensued. Champlain says: "Ours commenced, calling me in a loud voice, and, making way for me, opened in two, and placed me at their head, marching about 20 paces in advance until I was within 30 paces of the enemy. The moment they saw me they halted, gazing at me and I at them. When I saw them preparing to shoot at us, I raised my arquebus, and aiming directly at one of the three chiefs, two of them fell to the ground by this shot, and one of their companions received a wound, of which he died afterward. I had put four balls in my arquebus. Ours, in witnessing a shot so favorable to them, set up such tremendous shouts that thunder could not have been heard; and yet there was no lack of arrows on one side and the other. The Iroquois were greatly astonished, seeing two men killed so instantaneously, notwithstanding they were provided with arrow-proof armor, woven of cotton-thread and wood. . . . They lost courage, took to flight, and abandoned the field and their fort, hiding themselves in the depths of the forests; whither pursuing them I killed some others. . . . The place where the battle was fought is 43 degrees some minutes north latitude, and I named it Lake Champlain." Ticonderoga is 13½ degrees north latitude, and probably the cape referred to "which puts out into the lake on the west side." The French claimed the country by virtue of Champlain's discovery, and in 1731, while at peace with Great Britain, they advanced to Crown Point and erected Fort St. Frederick.

The English claimed this territory by right of purchase and treaty with the Five Nations. General Johnson was sent, in 1755, to drive the French from Crown Point, but halted at Lake George, when Baron Dieskau made his famous dash around French Mountain, defeated Colonel Williams, and attacked the main army, to be defeated in turn. He then retreated to Ticonderoga, and began the erection of a fort, which he called "*Carillon.*"

In 1757, somewhat enlarged, it was occupied by Montcalm, who marched thence to the capture of Fort William Henry. In 1758 Abercrombie made his unsuccessful attack on the old French lines, which resulted in his total defeat, with a loss of nearly 2,000 killed and wounded. The following year Amherst entrenched before them, and the French, satisfied that they could not successfully resist him, abandoned and set fire to the works, and the English took possession in the morning. The English advanced on Fort St. Frederick, the French retreated into Canada.

Amherst repaired and enlarged the works at Ticonderoga and Crown Point on a scale of great magnificence, but never after was a shot from the frowning embrasures directed against an approaching foe. Peace between the nations soon followed and the forts were allowed to fall into a state of ill repair and were poorly garrisoned when the revolution broke out. Ticonderoga had but 50 men, all told,

FORT TICONDEROGA.

when in the gray of the morning of the 10th of May, 1775, Ethan Allen and 83 of his "Green Mountain Boys" stole in through the wicket gate and demanded its surrender "in the name of the Great Jehovah and the Continental Congress."

In 1777 the brilliant general Burgoyne with 7,500 men came from the north and laid siege to Ticonderoga. St. Clair, who was then in command, had barely sufficient troops to man the principal works, and when the English took possession of Mt. Defiance, from which they could drop shot right over into their midst, he abandoned the fort, stealing away on the night of July 4th.

After the capture of Burgoyne at Saratoga, the British retired into Canada, but in 1780 the old fort was again occupied by the troops under General Haldiman. Then came another enemy, silent, but resistless as the march of time—frosts to rack and tempests to beat upon the old walls, until they totter and fall away, disappearing one by one, and bringing the time when naught shall remain but the name it bears, and that uncertain.

TICONDEROGA is the generally accepted composite of a dozen or more Indian terms applied to the place, all with something of the same sound, as *Tienderoga*, *Cheonderoga*, etc., the words used by the natives meaning the *coming together* or *meeting of waters** instead of the commonly given version of "sounding waters." Carillon, the name given it by the French, meaning "music racket, a chime," may have been suggested by the sounding waters of the falls at the outlet of Lake George, two miles distant.

---
* Colden, 1765. Pownell, 1774.

The old battery on the bluff, above the fort steamboat landing, is said to have been the original Carillon. Back on the higher ground are the barrack walls, trenches and bastions. On the west, beyond the outlet of Lake George, is Mount Defiance. Opposite the fort at the southeast, the lake is narrowed down by the near approach of Mount Independence, which was also fortified while St. Clair held command. Between the two points ran the chain, or floating bridge.

The lake here turns toward the north, thus washing three sides of the promontory. Among the oaks, just west of the tunnel, is the old French lines, reaching over the ridge and nearly across the peninsula. The trenches, embankments and two or three redoubts are clearly defined. Across the locust-covered flat, just north of the ruins, from a point near the drawbridge, lay Ethan Allen's route in 1775.

4. CROWN POINT is 11 miles north of Ticonderoga. On the lake-shore, are the furnaces of the Crown Point Iron Company, and the eastern terminus of a narrow-gauge railway, which extends back 13 miles to iron mines at Hammondville, 1,300 feet above the lake.

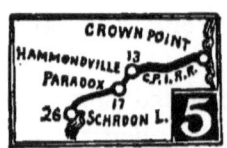

5. FORT FREDERICK is the landing at Crown Point Ruins, about 6 miles north of Crown Point village. The steamboat lands here on regular trips. The grounds have been fitted up by the Champlain Transportation Company for the accommodation of picnic parties that are brought here by their steamboats, with a dancing pavilion, refreshment rooms,

platforms and open spaces for games, swings, and other innocent accessories to sport. The lake is here narrowed down by the land on which the ruins stand, on the west side, the point marked by a stone light-house, and by Chimney Point, approaching

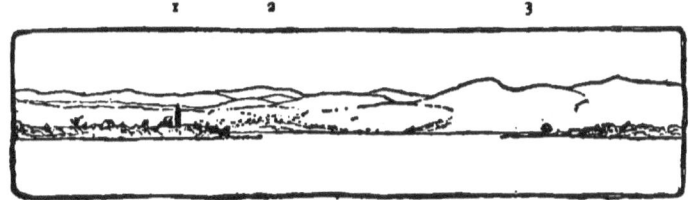

APPROACHING CROWN POINT RUINS FROM THE SOUTH.
1 Crown Point Light House ; 2 Port Henry ; 3 Chimney Point.

from the east. At the narrowest point in the passage, are the scarcely visible ruins of Fort St. Frederick, built by the French in 1731. This point became a noted trading post at that time, the savages coming to exchange peltry for civilized fire-water and other necessaries. Under the protecting guns of the old fort it developed into a village of 1,500 inhabitants. Remains of cellars and flagged walks, extending back toward the west, still show signs of its old-time prosperity.

CROWN POINT RUINS are over at the west. The walls of stone barracks are still in a good state of preservation, and the extensive earthworks indicate the magnitude of the fortifications. They were commenced by Amherst in 1759, and completed at an expense of ten million dollars, but never was a shot fired from them at an approaching enemy. When Ethan Allen captured Fort Ticonderoga, Crown Point was garrisoned only by a sergeant and 12 men, and was taken possession of by a part of

Allen's men under Seth Warner. In 1777 it was occupied by Burgoyne in his triumphant march south—triumphant until he reached Saratoga.

BULWAGA BAY is at the west, over beyond the peninsula on which the ruins stand. Dr. Geo. F. Bixby, of Plattsburgh, whose researches have confirmed, or proved the falsity of, many popular beliefs concerning the early history of the Champlain Valley, believes the shores of the peninsular just west of Crown Point Ruins to be the place where Champlain encountered the Iroquois to their confusion; and the cape referred to by him "which puts out into the lake on the west side."

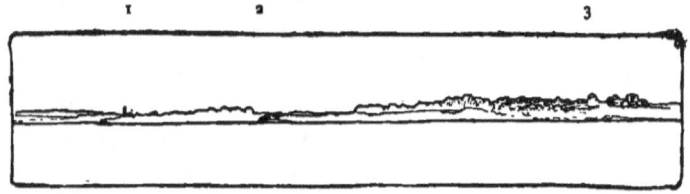

CROWN POINT FROM THE NORTH.
1 Crown Point Light House; 2 Ruins of Old Fort St. Frederick; 3 Ruins of Crown Point Barracks.

6. PORT HENRY, two miles north-west of Crown Point ruins, is exceedingly picturesque. It extends from the lake shore well up on the side of the mountain that rises boldly beyond, and has a number of elegant private residences, occupied by the iron magnates of that section, with churches, public schools, a pretty opera house, etc. The Lee House furnishes very good accommodations.

THE LAKE CHAMPLAIN AND MORIAH R. R. is seven miles long, extending from Port Henry to the ore beds at Mineville, 1,300 feet above. The grade is neces-

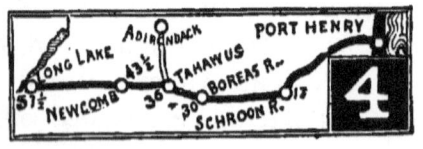

sarily heavy. At one point it is 256½ feet to the mile. The average is 211 feet. The grade contains three "Ys," where the nature of the ascent renders a curve impracticable. By plank-road Mineville is but five miles from the lake.

7. THE CHEVER ORE BED is two miles north of Port Henry, near the lake shore.

8. The Y M. C. A. of Albany, has a summer camp on No-Man's Island, west shore, a mile south of Barber Point light house. Rules require, obedience to leader, attendance at Bible Study, quiet at 10 P. M.

9. WESTPORT is a pretty little village, on a deep bay setting into the western shore, fifty miles north of Whitehall. It is the natural gateway into the mountains, *via* Elizabethtown and Keene Valley, and possesses attractions of its own that recommend it strongly to the summer visitor.

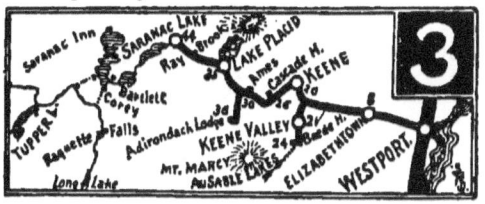

THE WESTPORT INN, overlooking the steamboat landing, is under the management of Mrs. O. C. Daniell and Mrs. Henry C. Lyon. Capacity 50. Rates, $3 per day. This is an excellent house.

THE GIBBS HOUSE, formerly Richards House, is at the northern border of the village. Capacity 40. Rates, $2 per day; $8 to $14 per week. N. J. Gibbs, proprietor.

THE "WATER LILY," a small steamboat, runs from Westport to Vergennes daily, on arrival of the steamer Vermont from the south, returning in the morning to connect with the south bound boat.

The Water Lily is notable among steamboats as having a lady at the wheel, in the person of Mrs. Captain Daniels, who is said to be the first and only regularly licensed lady pilot in the United States. Fare, $1.00. Round trip, $1.50.

STEAMER CHATEAUGAY, Capt. Baldwin, leaves this point at 7:00 A. M. daily, Sundays excepted, and touching at Cedar Bay, Burlington, Plattsburgh and intermediate points, arrives at North Hero at 12:15. Returning over the same course reaches Essex at 6.00 P. M. This boat belongs to the C. T. Co., and was launched at Shelburne Harbor, November 1, 1887. It is 203 feet long, and 59 feet wide over all. Water line, 195 feet ; beam, 30 feet. The hull is of rolled steel plates, made from Chateaugay ore, with a wrought iron frame, braced in the most substantial manner, and provided with water-tight compartments. The engine is a vertical-beam, jet condensing engine, 44-inch cylinder, 10 ft. stroke. The paddle-wheels are of the new "feathering" pattern, 23 feet in diameter. The boat draws four and a half feet of water, and will make 20 miles an hour.

10. CALAMITY POINT is on the west, about two miles north of Westport. Here the luckless steamer Champlain was wrecked in 1875 while running north on her regular night trip. The immediate cause of the disaster has never been explained, as the night was no more than ordinarily dark, but since that time, day or night when running, the pilot houses of the sister boats invariably contain two competent men. Captain Rushlow of the Vermont was then in command of the Champlain, and it was due to his self-possession that no panic ensued to lead to

loss of life. Her engine now does efficient service in the graceful "Horicon" on Lake George.

11. Split Rock Mountain extends along the west shore terminating in a sharp point 8 miles north of Westport. The sides toward the lake, close under which the steamer runs at times, are precipitous, and at points wild and grand. Barn Rock (a corruption probably of Barren Rock) shows the upturned edges of strata lying at a sharp angle with the surface in a bold point enclosing a deep harbor. "The Palisades," a little way north, are grand perpendicular cliffs. Rock Harbor, a mile further north, shows an "effort," where Gotham's ex-Boss, Tweed, tried his hand at digging ore. Openings are to be seen in the mountain side, with piles of ore below, and the buildings high up in the notch beyond. Grog Harbor—a charming little cove despite its name—is near the northern end of the mountain.

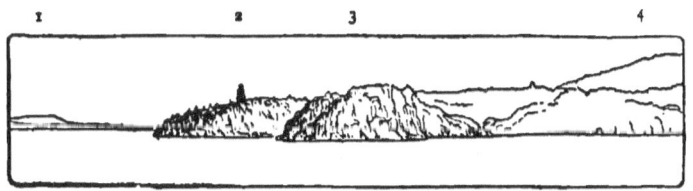

SPLIT ROCK FROM THE NORTH.
1 Grand View Mt., Vt.; 2 Split Rock Light ; 3 Split Rock ; 4 Whalon's Bay.

Split Rock is at the northern termination of the mountain bearing the same name. It is a rough fragment, perhaps a half acre in area, separated from the main land by a narrow passage. In the uncertain records of old Indian treaties, it is claimed that this rock marked the line between the tribes of the St. Lawrence and those of the Mohawk Valley. It also divides the honor of being the ancient " Rock Regio " with Rock Dunder, lying just south of Burlington. It was the unremovable monument set up by the treaty of Utrecht in 1710 to indicate the line between English and French possessions, and later accepted as the northern boundary of New York, but in the rearrangement of the geographies in the school of 1775 and 1776, the line drifted some sixty miles further north.

12. OTTER CREEK enters the lake from the east, something over five miles north of Westport. This is the longest river, or creek, in Vermont, and is navigable to Vergennes, whose spires may be seen some distance inland.

FORT CASSIN was built at the mouth of Otter Creek, and some of the works are still visible. Within the creek a portion of the American squadron was fitted out in 1814, which, under Commodore McDonough, defeated the British Commodore Downie at Plattsburgh in September of that year.

VERGENNES, is eight miles back from the lake, following the course of the river, although in an airline but little more than half of that distance. Vergennes is one of the oldest cities in New England, dating its organization back to 1789, and is celebrated as the smallest incorporated city in the country. It has a population of about 2,000 inhabitants, with all the honors and added dignity of a mayor and board of aldermen.

THE STEVENS HOUSE, owned and under the management of Mr. S. S. Gaines, has accommodations for about 100 guests. Telegraph, telephone and express offices are in the house. Board costs from $8 to $12 per week.

LAKE CHAMPLAIN. 109

13. CEDAR BEACH, on the Vermont shore, nearly opposite Split Rock, is a village of cottage-camps owned principally by residents of Burlington.

14. ESSEX, a small village on the west shore, is 10 miles north of Westport.

15. THE BOUQUET RIVER empties into the lake four miles north of Essex landing. It is navigable for about a mile. It was a rendezvous of Burgoyne's flotilla in his advance on Ticonderoga in 1777, and in 1812 was entered by British gunboats to work the destruction of the little village of Willsborough lying a mile inland.

16. THE WILLSBOROUGH stands near the northern extremity of Willsborough Point, a low peninsula about four miles long by one wide separating Willsborough Bay from the main lake. The house has capacity for 100 guests. J. Henry Otis, proprietor. P. O., Willsborough Point. Rates, $3.00 per day; $12 to $18 per week. Open June to October. The accommodations here are all that can be reasonably desired, except that they are not sufficient for the demand, and during July and August would-be guests will do well to engage rooms in advance.

Steamer Chateaugay lands daily. Railroad station is Willsborough, five miles distant. Notice should be sent in advance to assure attendance of carriage on arrival of train.

THE AMERICAN CANOE ASSOCIATION holds its annual meet again this year on the north end of Willsborough Point, August 4th to 25th inclusive. This is an international organization with a membership of over a thousand and is composed largely of literary and professional men. The Association is bound by a code of rules that keeps it free from what may be termed "professionalism." Its official organs are "*Forest and Stream*" and "*Rudder, Sail and Paddle.*" The initiationfee is one dollar, annual dues one dollar. Charles V. Winne of Albany, Commodore; W. B. Wackerhagen, Albany, Secretary and Treasurer.

The Association is divided into four divisions, Eastern, Northern, Atlantic and Southern. E. L. French, of Buffalo, is Vice-Commodore, and C. C. Belman of Amsterdam, Purser, of the Central Division, in whose jurisdiction the Meet is held this year. The A. C. A. was organized at Lake George in 1880, and has met annually since that time at Lake George and other places. The camp is under strict police surveillance and strangers are not allowed on the grounds except under certain restrictions and on regular visitors' day, at which time it is intended that some of the most interesting events of the Meet shall transpire.

17. THE FOUR BROTHERS are near the middle of the lake, east of Willsborough Point. Here occurred the running engagement between Benedict Arnold and Capt. Pringle, in 1776, in which the English were victorious.

18. JUNIPER ISLAND is northeast of the Brothers, with high, almost vertical walls, and surmounted by a light-house.

After leaving Essex Landing the boat passes out into the broadening lake gradually nearing the Vermont side in the approach to Burlington. Back inland are the two highest peaks of the Green

Mountains—Mansfield, 4,350 feet above tide, and Camel's Hump, the *Leon Couchant* of the French.

19. ROCK DUNDER is a prominent object, as we near Burlington. It is a sharp cone about 20 feet high, believed by Winslow C. Watson, the historian, to be the famous "Rock Regio," so frequently mentioned in colonial records, notwithstanding the counter-claims of Split Rock. The steamer usually passes close by on its east side. Pottier's Point terminates a long stretch of regular shore on the right.

20. SHELBURNE HARBOR is east of Pottier's Point. Here are the ship-yards of the Champlain Transportation Company, and here have been built all the large boats of Lake Champlain. It is worthy of note that but one year after Robert Fulton's first steamboat was launched on the Hudson River a steamboat was built and launched at Burlington. And it could run 5 miles an hour without heating the shaft, too.

LA PLOTTE river empties into Shelburne Harbor. It is said its name was bestowed because of an incident of the Revolution. It appears that a party of Indians had left their canoes unguarded on the banks while making a raid on the scattered settlement beyond. They were finally driven back by the whites and took to their canoes for safety, but the canoes had been discovered by some prying settlers and riddled with holes which let the water in, and the settlers now proceeded to riddle the savages also. The Green Mountain Boys were very artistic about these little affairs.

several hundred acres along the shore of the lake, and is credited with looking still for more.

21. BURLINGTON is a beautiful city of nearly 15,000 inhabitants, 80 miles north of Whitehall. It is one of the largest lumber marts in the country, standing fourth in the order of business. The firms representing a capital of $4,000,000,00. 150,000,000 feet of lumber are sold annually from the markets.

Three railroads centre here—the Central Vermont, the Burlington & Lamoille, and the Rutland & Burlington railroad.

The Champlain Transportation Company has its general offices here, its steamers running to connect with the D. & H. trains on the west shore, and to Adirondack points.

The University of Vermont is located here—crowning the hill, on the western slope of which, the principal part of the city lies. Among other public buildings of interest are the Medical College, Billings Library building, Vermont Episcopal Institute, St. Joseph's College, Park Gallery of Art, Fletcher Free Library, the Mary Fletcher Hospital, and the Young Men's Christian Association building. Joined to the last is the book store of S. Huntington & Co., which is one of the most complete in appointments of any store devoted to this business, outside the great cities of the country.

On the high land, back of the city, overlooking Winooski Valley, is the Green Mountain Cemetery, where lies the body of Vermont's famous son, Ethan Allen. A monument of Barre granite, 50 feet in height, surmounted by a statue of Allen, marks the spot, and is a shrine often visited by admirers of the Hero of Ticonderoga.

LAKE CHAMPLAIN. 113

HOTELS are Hotel Burlington, Delaney & Harrington, proprietors. Rates, $2.00 and $2.50 per day; and the VAN NESS and AMERICAN HOUSES, U. A. Woodbury, proprietor, H. N. Clark, manager. Rates, $3.00 and $3.50 per day.

22. COLCHESTER POINT reaches out half way across the broad lake north of Burlington, and still further west are Colchester reef and light-house, a blood-red light marking the outermost rock at night.

23. SCHUYLER ISLAND is a large cultivated island lying near the west shore. Trembleau Mountain is beyond, terminating at Trembleau Point.

24. PORT KENT is 10 miles from Burlington. Below, the town is not attractive; but above, along

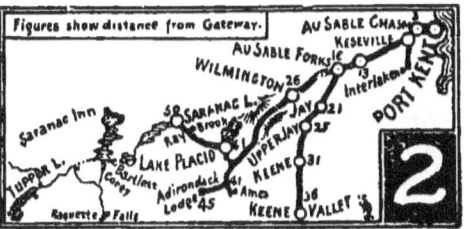

the brow of the hills are several very pleasant, comfortable looking houses, among them the old home of Elkanah Watson, the historian.

Trembleau Hall, a boarding house, with capacity for about 20 guests, has been opened recently by Farrel & Adgate. Rates unknown.

The Keeseville, Au Sable Chasm and Lake Champlain Railroad runs from Port Kent to Keeseville, passing over *the* chasm a short distance below beautiful Rainbow falls. It is five miles long and was built primarily in the interests of the Au Sable Horse Nail words at Keeseville, for the transportation of the material used in their extensive works.

THE GRAND FLUME.

This is the point of departure for Au Sable Chasm and the interior, *via* the Au Sable Valley.

AU SABLE CHASM is the Yosemite in miniature. The Au Sable River, coming out from the mountains of the south, through the valley past Keeseville, breaks, after many a rush and tumble, over the rocks into Au Sable Chasm, in the beautiful Rainbow Falls, then hurrying downward through devious ways, creeping under towering cliffs, resting in dark places where the sun never shines, finally emerges from the gloom into the broad willowy way to mingle later, after many twists and turns, with the quiet waters of Lake Champlain.

It is a vast fissure in the Earth's surface, its walls that now stand apart, were apparently united and solid in the past; projections on the one side are faced by corresponding depressions on the other; strata broken off here are continued over there. Low down are found petrified specimens of the first orders of animal life and ripple marks made when the rock was in its plastic state—the bed of some lake or ocean—and above these, in successive layers, towers nearly a hundred feet of solid rock.

Who can say what ages have passed away since the restless sea beat upon this unknown shore and left the marks of its wavelets for us to wonder at? Thought is lost away back in the eternity of "The Beginning" when darkness was upon the face of the deep. Later came the dawn of Creation, and in its full light the lowest of animal creatures lived their brief day and added their mite to old Ocean's bottom. Long ages rolled away. Floods swept over the uneasy world that reeled and staggered with the pulsations of its heart of fire. The Earth's thin shell bubbled up into mountain ridges and broke like crackle glass, then, cooling, left its marks in ragged heights and fearful depths. Then came great icebergs, grinding the uplifted points to atoms in their course, polishing, leveling and filling up the openings. Then the water fled away, leaving the seams and cracks filled with a rich alluvium gathered in passing centuries, holding in its bosom the germs of vegetable life that in time covered all with a mantle of green. The yearly rains descended, floods swept down from the mountains above, washing outward the loose deposit and the softer rock that had filled these crevices, and revealing to us this wonderland of " The Walled Banks of the Au Sable."

In 1873 a number of gentlemen from Philadelphia, under the corporative name of The Ausable Company, acquired the land lying along the west side, with an entrance and an exit on the east, and built stairways, galleries and bridges, which, with the aid of boats near the lower end, enabled visitors to pass entirely through the chasm. In 1879 the old wooden galleries were replaced by stone walks with substantial iron railings, bridges were erected above high water mark, or made movable so as to be taken up at the close of the season, and put back in the spring, and new boats were placed in the navigable waters below Table Rock, to carry visitors through the otherwise inaccessable portions of the gorge. The admission to the chasm is 50 cents; the boat ride 50 cents additional. The boats are in charge of experienced men, and although exciting, the ride is attended with no danger, so the most timid need not hestitate in going.

LAKE CHAMPLAIN.   119

THE LAKE VIEW HOUSE overlooks the head of the Chasm from the east. Capacity 100. Rates, $2.50 per day; special for week or season; open June 1st to October 15th. P. O., Au Sable Chasm. W. H. Tracy proprietor. The main structure was burnt last spring but a smaller one was promptly erected to take its place. The dining capacity is practically unlimited The hotel and Chasm are under one management and Mr. Tracy should be addressed for particulars relating to either. The admission fee to the Chasm depends upon circumstances; large parties are admitted at reduced rates; guests of the Lake View have free access. Guides are unnecessary, as once in the Chasm, the course is plain, guide boards and signs pointing the way and calling attention to notable places until Table Rock is reached where boats are entered for the remainder of the trip. Stop-over privileges are given passengers by rail and boat at Port Kent. The hotel carriage conveys guests to and from the Chasm station for 25 cents the round trip.

Admission to the Chasm is gained through "The Lodge," a picturesque building, octagonal in form, pagoda-like, unique and attractive. Within, will be found photographs, books and curios pertaining to the place. Before descending, note the queer effect the stained glass in the lodge windows, give to objects seen through them, where the blue makes frosty winter, and the red the most insufferable of summers of the same objects.

RAINBOW FALLS, at the head of the Chasm, flings its mass of water from nearly 70 feet above into the gulf below. Horse Shoe Falls is nearly opposite

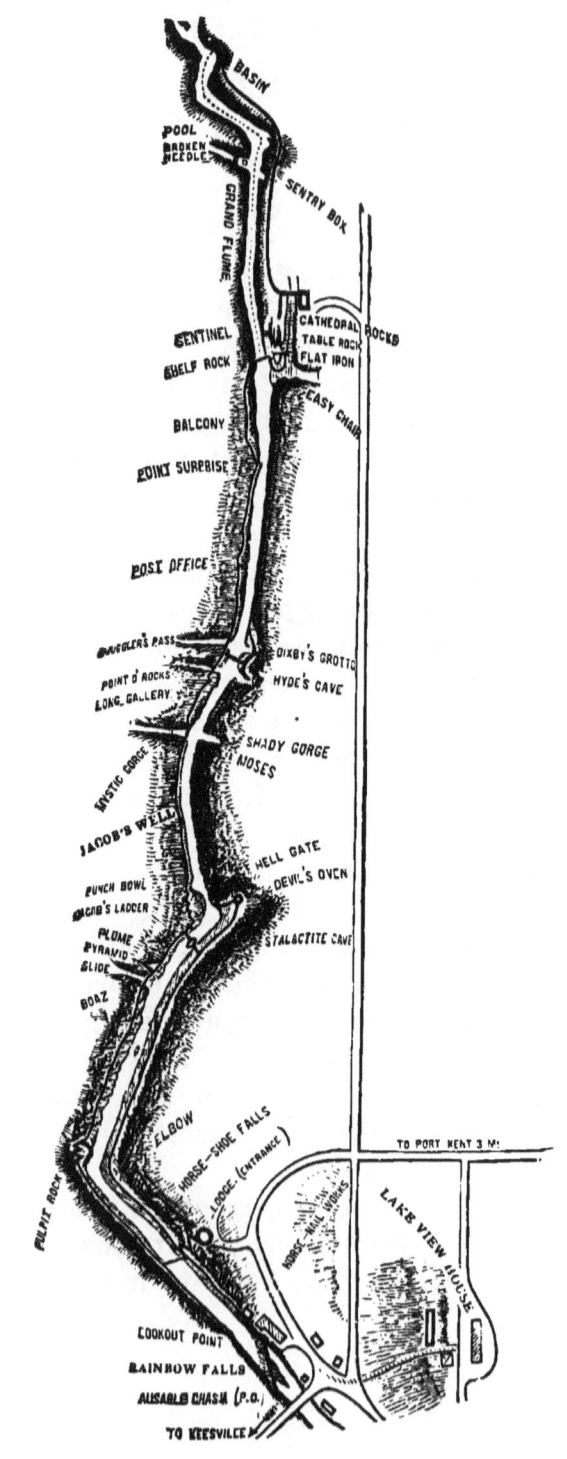

the entrance. Note its suggestive shape from the lookout, before descending the stairs.

PULPIT ROCK faces us as we approach the Elbow, which is the first turn below the entrance. Split Rock shows on the left at the farthest point visible as you turn around the Elbow. The rock which stands at the left of the opening made by the splitting off of a large fallen mass is called the Elephant's Head and with the morning sun lighting up the massive front, the name does not seem inappropriate.

Stop when you reach the end of the bridge that crosses here. The Devil's Oven is in the wall which shuts off our farther advance on the right of the stream. Why "Oven" is not so clear, for if you climb the rough rocks and enter its 30 feet of depth, you will not find it the superheated place suggested, but rather the reverse. The same tropical imagination that conceived of this and some of the other names applied to places here, gave to the narrow passage-way at our feet the name of Hell Gate, and looking, one does not really wonder at the fancy. From Hell Gate, rising in a great sweep heavenward, away from the rushing waters, is Jacob's Ladder.

Across the bridge we go, around the rocky abutment toward the left, clinging perhaps to the iron railing which prevents our sliding into the water below, beneath overhanging rocks, over the seething water, across the bridge which spans the Devil's Punch-Bowl—pausing, perhaps, to glance into the green depths of the Fernery at our left—down across the worn rocks, then zig-zag up the side to a higher level. Here is one of the most remarkable, specimens of rock boring in the country, called

THE SENTINEL.

Jacob's Well, showing where some vagrant stone, caught, perhaps, in an eddy when the stream ran here, and whirled away continually, ground its way down through the strata of soft rock, until it wore itself out in vain beatings against its prison walls. Here a bridge crosses Mystic Gorge, to the Long Gallery beyond which, descending, we come to Point of Rocks. Note high up the sides of those rocks the segments of a large bowl similar to Jacob's Well, and backward the rapids which, seen from this point, in the sunshine at noon, are very beautiful. Opposite this point is Hyde's Cave, named after a venturesome individual, who, in 1871, let himself down by a rope from the rocks above and was the first to reach its dual entrance. Below the bridge, which leads to Hyde's Cave, on the same side of the stream, is Bixby's Grotto.

Returning to the north shore, Smuggler's Pass, directly opposite the Grotto, is crossed by a bridge. You may follow along the ledge if you like and lose yourself from sight where, back from the river, this passage winds into quite a large chamber. More stairways are found as we proceed, then comes the Post Office. This post office has neither post master nor distinguishing name in the postal department, but nevertheless does a large business, peculiarly its own, as the observant visitor will notice. No charge is made here for drop-letter or cards, and many avail themselves of the privilege.

Clinging close to the rocks protected by the iron railing we pass along high up at this point, then through the Hanging Garden, and, descending, cross to Table Rock.

From the upper point of Table Rock look backward through the Upper Flume. See Column Rocks at the farthest visible point on the left, and, if the sun be right, notice the Altar-cloth hanging over the water at the right. Turning, the Anvil is before you; partially hidden, perhaps, by the rustic canopy which has been built against it to afford shade for such as may care to take advantage of it when, for two or three brief hours in the middle of the day, the sun pours its beams down into this open space. Back of the Anvil, Cathedral Rocks rise a hundred feet above the level floor, suggesting in their broken lines, some vast cathedral's ruined towers and aisles. "The Sentinel" stands guard at the outer corner of Cathedral Rocks.

Through a cleft in the lower edge of Table Rock we descend and enter the large batteaux found waiting here for the passage through the Grand Flume and beyond. Do not fear, for these boats are strong and serviceable, to withstand the hard knocks they get at times, and in charge of stalwart boatmen who will guide us safely through the exciting passage below. The Grand Flume reaches from Table Rock for some distance down. Here the water runs straight away, shut in by walls that rise perpendicularly up for more than a hundred feet, while the dip of the rock-strata on either side gives one the queer sensation of running down quite a steep hill.

Here, at the narrowest place, the cliffs are scarcely ten feet apart, and the sky above seems but a narrow ribbon of blue. The water seems to round up in the middle and actually to run on edge. No plummet has ever been found to sound its depths. Over this spot the main road crossed years ago, and the place is spoken of now by the older inhabitants as "High Bridge." A story is told to the effect that when after a time the bridge was condemned and the plank taken off leaving only the naked log stringers stretched across, a horseman went across one dark and stormy night, unconscious of his danger at the time, although remembering afterward that as he approached in the intense darkness, his horse had hesitated, and when urged moved forward in fear and trembling.

The Lower Gate-Way ends the Long Flume and ushers us into the Pool. The Sentry Box is at the right as we emerge into the open space. On the left there is a larger *crevasse* in which, leaning, stands the Broken Needle. At the Pool, the river turns sharply to the left and leads downward over dancing rapids where we go until, rounding to the right, we enter quiet water once more, and finally pass out into the basin where, at the landing, carriages are taken to convey us back to the hotel.

It is well to have passed through Au Sable Chasm once in a life time. Such scenes make man realize the puny creature that he is, for—in the somewhat stalwart language of Will Carleton:

"——To appreciate Heaven well
It is good for a man to have some fifteen minutes of Hell."

25.—Three miles north of the landing at Port Kent, is the sandy mouth of the Ausable River which is supposed to have suggested its name, Ausable meaning "a river of sand." A wooded depression in the ground above shows the course of the river. Across from this is the widest uninterrupted portion of the lake, being here a little more than ten miles in width. Measuring down into Mallett's bay brings the distance to about 13 miles.

26. VALCOUR ISLAND is about six miles north of Port Kent, the steamer passing between it and the main land on the west. Here, Oct. 11, 1776, occurred the first naval engagement of the Revolution, between the British, commanded by Captain Thomas Pringle, and the Americans under Benedict Arnold. The British plan was to send a fleet from the north to capture Ticonderoga and clear the way for a junction with the army of the south, that should come by way of the Hudson. Early in the spring they began the construction of ships at St. Johns, and the last of September the fleet—consisting of a three-masted vessel carrying eighteen guns, and two schooners with thirteen guns each, with smaller vessels, twenty-nine vessels in all, mounting eighty-nine guns, manned by picked seamen and practiced gunners—moved south to the attack. When it became known that preparations of this nature were in progress at St. Johns, Arnold was commissioned to construct vessels to oppose them. Massing all possible help and material at Skenesborough (now Whitehall), he set about the work with tremendous energy, and in August put afloat a number of flat-bottomed sailing craft and row galleys, carrying altogether 84 guns and 152 swivel-guns. The largest of these vessels was the "Royal Savage," a two-masted schooner carrying fourteen guns. With this force Arnold sailed north, going as far as Windmill Point, then returning, took up a position in the narrow channel between Valcour Island and the main land.

The British fleet, running before the strong **north**

wind, passed on the outside of the island and some distance beyond, before discovering the position of the Americans. So severe was the wind that the larger vessels could not be brought back to attack and only some of the smaller ones with the schooner, Carleton, finally succeeded in getting into position. The engagement continued most of the afternoon during which the "Royal Savage" was disabled, and drifting on the rocks was abandoned. During the night it was set on fire by the British and sunk. Portions of the hull can yet be seen when the water is still, resting on the bottom where it then went down. The attacking vessels were recalled and anchored in line at the south, to cut off the retreat of the Americans. During the night, however, the Americans slipped through the British line and in the morning were discovered making industrious tracks toward the south and safety. The British pursuing, overhauled Arnold near the Four Brothers and a running fight ensued which demonstrated the superiority of the British vessels and gunners. The remnant of the American boats, almost disabled, was grounded in a bay on the Vermont shore near Panton and set on fire, and Arnold and his men made their way through the woods to Crown Point. In these engagements, although defeated, Arnold acquitted himself in such a manner as to win the admiration of his enemies and the approval of his superior officers. Benedict Arnold was born in Norwich, Conn., Jan. 3d, 1741, and died in London, June 14, 1801. As a youth, turbulent; as a soldier, ambitious, bold to rashness and jealous of his fellow officers; dishonest; the transition from discontented rebel to infamous traitor was easy. He was a brilliant commander—his fall was like that of Lucifer.

Valcour Island was the spot selected for "a communal home, based on the principles of social science," where the "Dawn Valcour Community" dawned on the astonished world of 1874, grew into a mighty power (on paper), with "Col." John Wilcox to furnish the intellectual, and "Uncle" Owen Shipman the temporal home; where congenial spirits were invited to commingle in promiscuity, but all too soon were on the ragged edge of individuality, while the musical auctioneer warbled over the odds and ends that remained to satisfy outside demands. In the words of one of its leading members, the thing "busted;" and the "Dawn" was merged into twilight, to furnish another lesson on the practicability of free love.

27. Hotel Champlain, the superb, is seen on the bold headland that puts out from the west shore just north of Valcour Island. It does not come upon you suddenly, as a revelation. You have seen it over the lake for miles back on your course, before the steamer had touched at Burlington, perhaps, or from the car window as the reeling train swung around Trembleau Mountain nearly ten miles away, and at intervals ever since as the road wound in and out along the shore. Now, as you approach, its magnificent proportions come out in grand relief against the sky.

"Commanding" is not misapplied here. The hotel stands on a height that breaks away abruptly in all directions for a space, then in gentler slope reaches the level of the lower shores north and south, the water on the east, and the valley toward the west where the trains on the D. & H. flash like gleaming shuttles through the vari-tinted web of cultivated fields and cross-line country roads. Long colonades; broad piazzas conforming to the swelling contour of facing, east, south and west; breezy porticos, and balconies, hung along its sides or perched high up on tower and sharply sloping roof, give grace and lightness to the structure that rises above the tops of the trees crowning the rugged bluff. Distance gives to it the lightness of a castle built of straws, the closer view reveals it solid and substantial as the most realistic could wish.

At a moderate elevation it commands in an unbroken circuit a panorama that for picturesque variety and beauty is equaled perhaps nowhere in the country. Having no near mountain heights to dwarf its own strong setting, it looks out from its own native wilderness over land and water diversified and changeful. It is restful, rather than overpowering with great heights and dismal depths. Right and left runs the valley with its checker-board of field and woodland; its network of roads; its quaint farm buildings gathered here and there in little knots that form hamlets and prosperous villages, and beyond, hills rising into the ranges of the Adirondacks that stretch across, pointed at intervals with the grander mountain peaks. Toward the southeast a splendid road winds through the trees to the dock where busy life attends as the steamers come and go. East a broad swathe has been cut out through the green trees down to the water's edge, where gleam the beach of "The Singing Sands" circling in a broad belt toward the south, between the restless water and the thick growing cedars.

Towards the north are perpendicular cliffs that attain quite a height — the bluffs which undoubtedly gave to the point its name. They are cleft asunder at one place and made memorable by the tradition of the White Squaw and the Bloody Hand that left its marks on the walls, and later as the place where smugglers successfully landed their stores free from suspicion because of its seeming inaccessibility, to those who were not in the secret.

Valcour island lies like a garden below, bordered with its varying belt of shrubbery. Beyond stretches the broad lake, dotted here and there with islands to the shores of Vermont, the Green Mountains beyond rising into the heights of Camel's Hump and Mount Mansfield. North and east are Grand Isle and the Great Back Bay; at the north Cumberland Head, the sweeping circle of Plattsburgh Bay where occurred that splendid naval battle of 1814—the last, as the battle of Valcour was the first, with the mother country—and nearer, the little island where sleep the dead of that eventful day.

Within the hotel is found everything that appertains to a — oh, much, an ill-used term — first-class house. Every modern appliance tending to the comfort of guests will be found here. Its management will undoubtedly be all which time and experience has shown to be the most acceptable to the travelled public, for O. D. Seavey, of the Ponce de Leon, St. Augustine, Florida, is at its head.

Excursions may be made by steamboat from this point south to Ticonderoga or north among the islands and on to the fishing grounds of the Lake. A fleet of boats, ranging from the light Whitehall skiff to the dainty little steam yacht, are here for charter. Drives are many and varied, and equipages here to suit all occasions. The distance from New York is 308 miles; fare $8.05. To montreal, 77 miles; fare

D. & H. RAILROAD STATION.

$2.71. Quick and convenient train service will be maintained throughout the season north and south. Trains on the Chateaugay Railroad leave in the morning, arriving at Saranac Lake and the various hotels reached by the Chateaugay Railroad in time for dinner.

CRAB ISLAND, some distance north of Valcour, is the burial place of the common sailors and marines who fell in the battle of Plattsburgh. North of this, and projecting well out across the lake, is Cumberland Head, from which the shore recedes toward the north and west, then comes back in a wide sweep, embracing the waters of Cumberland Bay.

THE BATTLE OF PLATTSBURGH took place here in 1814. Stripped of detail, the account of this decisive battle is as follows: On a beautiful Sabbath morning, September 11th, 1814, the American land forces under General McComb, and the American fleet under Commodore Macdonough, were simultaneously attacked by the British land and water forces, under General Sir George Provost and Commodore Downie. The engagement resulted in a complete victory for the former, only a few small boats of the enemy effecting a successful retreat. At the commencement of the naval engagement, the British land forces, consisting of 14,000 infantry advanced against the Americans, 3,000 strong, entrenched at points along the south bank of the river, but were repulsed with a loss of 2,500 in killed, wounded and missing. They also lost immense stores, which were abandoned in their retreat—which served them right for breaking the Sabbath. The ruins of the old forts are to be seen on the south outskirts of the village. The largest—Fort Moreau —is in the centre, Fort Brown, on the bank of the river, and Fort Scott near the lake. Plattsburgh is a regular army post. The barracks, about a mile south of the village, near the lake shore, built in 1838, are occupied by a company of soldiers belonging to the regular army.

PLATTSBURGH is on the west shore of this bay, a thriving village of 8,000 inhabitants. It is of considerable commercial importance, being on the direct line between New York and Montreal, 311 miles from the former and 74 from the latter. It is the northern terminus of the Au Sable (Branch) Railroad, and from it the Chateaugay Railroad penetrates the mountains toward the west. Plattsburgh is thoroughly cosmopolitan, with an opinion to offer on every question of the day, exerting no mean influence through its wide-awake newspapers, the *Daily Telegram*, and the *Sentinel* and *Republican*— the latter instituted in 1811, and, notwithstanding its age, one of the most reliable and ably conducted democratic weeklies in the state.

The first settler in this region was Count Charles de Fredenburgh, a captain in the English army, The warrant conveying the land to him bore date June 11, 1769.

The property reverting to the state after the Revolution, was granted, in 1784, to Zephaniah Platt and others, and incorporated into the town of Plattsburgh, April 4, 1785. A company was then organized which, in June of the same year, erected a mill at Fredenburgh Falls. The estimate of expense contained among other items, the following: "For bread, $65; for rum $80." They used a great deal of bread in those days.

In the year 1800 Plattsburgh was the county seat, its territory extended from Lake George on the south to Canada and the St. Lawrence River on the north and west. The village then possessed a population of less than 300, and within the county limits were owned at this time 58 slaves.

THE FOUQUET HOUSE is at the depot, and affords a convenient stopping place for parties arriving late or desiring to take an early train out.

THE WITHERILL HOUSE is near the post-office. It is elegant in its appointments, its pictures and decorations displaying a high degree of artistic taste.

THE CUMBERLAND stands at the corner of Trinity Square. It is one of the oldest hotels, but has renewed its youth, and is in splendid condition under its new management. Rates, $2.50 per day. Charles F. Beck, late of the Florida House, St. Augustine, Florida, and of Hotel Champlain, Rouse's Point, is proprietor. A free bus runs to trains and boats, and ample time is given for breakfast here between the arrival of morning train from the south and departure of train for the interior.

There is also an excellent restaurant in the depot, under railroad management, where a good lunch can be had at a moderate price, or a really superior and well ordered meal during the twenty or more minutes given for that purpose between the arrival and departure of trains on the main line.

THE CHATEAUGAY RAILROAD extends from Plattsburgh to Saranac Lake, a distance of 73 miles. The first section was built by the State to reach Clinton Prison, at Dannemora, 17 miles from Plattsburgh. In 1880, it was extended to Lyon Mountain, 17 miles further; but the influx of Adirondack tourists was increased, and the road that climbed an altitude of 2,000 feet, to Lyon Mountain, must go farther into the wilderness. So it was extended to Loon Lake. In 1888, 19 miles more were added, bringing it to Saranac Lake, distributing its passengers by various stage routes that

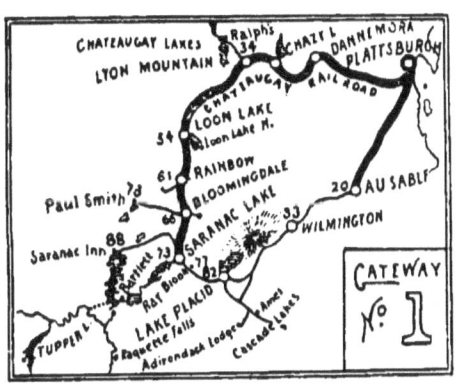

branch from it to a score or more of summer hotels. By it tourists reach Chazy, Chateaugay, Loon. Rainbow, St. Regis, and Upper and Lower Saranac Lakes, Ray Brook, Lake Placid, Mirror Lake, Cascade Lakes and Adirondack Lodge. A Wagner sleeping car leaves Grand Central station, New York, daily, the year round, for Plattsburgh, where passengers are given time for breakfast, before leaving for the interior. During the pleasure season, passengers can leave Grand Central Station at 7:30 P. M., connecting with trains leaving Plattsburgh 7:30 A. M., and reach the various resorts in time for dinner. Passengers can leave New York at 6 P. M., by Hudson River night boats and by the Adirondack special from Albany or Troy, reaching Plattsburgh at 12:20 and Saranac Lake 4:30 P. M., the following day. Sleeping and drawing-room car accommodations can be secured in advance at any of the stations. Drawing-room cars are run on all trains. A Sunday train each way will run during July and August connecting with sleeper for New York.

30. CUMBERLAND HEAD is three miles from Plattsburgh. Near it occurred the naval battle of 1814. Continuing northward the west shore is low but picturesque in its irregular line of deep bays and projecting points, but of little interest historically except for the old fort that once stood on Point au Fer, built, according to the best authorities, in 1774, then comes Rouse's Point.

31. ROUSES POINT, according to the United States Coast Survey, is about 107 miles north of Whitehall, although the deviation from the direct line made by the steamboat in reaching the various landings, increases the distance a number of miles.

It is a place of considerable commercial interest, and the most important port of entry on the frontier. Five railroads centre here, viz: The D. & H., leading to New York, the O. & L. C., to Ogdensburg and the Thousand Islands, the Grand Trunk to Montreal, the Portland & Ogdensburg to the White Mountains, and the Central Vermont to Boston and the southeast. There is a very good hotel at the station and another—Hotel Windsor—on the lake shore a half mile south of the village.

32. FORT MONTGOMERY, a little way north of the long bridge, is an interesting ruin belonging to the United States. About a mile north of this a belt of woodland marks the boundary line between the United States and Canada.

* * * * * *

THE ISLANDS of Lake Champlain lie principally in its northern and broader parts. The larger ones are North and South Hero and Isle La Motte, which, with others of less note, and with Alburgh Tongue—extending from the north centrally eleven miles south of the Dominion line—constitute Grand Isle county belonging to the State of Vermont. Concerning this section, that enthusiastic sportsman, Dr. George F. Bixby, editor of the Plattsburgh *Republican* says :

"Here are islands which now appear in their original beauty as when Champlain first saw them, the abode of eagles, so secluded are they. Here is better fishing, all the year round, than any other body of water in Northern New York can boast of; big, hungry fish, voracious pike, huge black bass, as well as the muscallonge—that nearly extinct fish—the noblest and gamiest that swims, ready for the fisherman at all seasons. In their season, water fowl abound—enormous black ducks and wild geese, with smaller game in abundance, while its facility of access from the Hudson and St. Lawrence for all kinds of craft; hospitality of inhabitants, pure air; pure water; delightful scenery, eligible camping grounds and abundant bases of supplies, all offer irresistible attraction to those unable to endure the fatigue incident to a lodge in the vast wilderness, or that other class who are 'constitutionally tired.'"

In proof of the Doctor's faith in his own medicine is "Eagle Reef Lodge" on the North Sister, where lucky friend or luckless castaway may, alike, feel certain of a hearty welcome.

SOUTH HERO, the largest of the islands, is twelve miles long and fills about one-third of the width of the lake. It is reached from the west by steamer, to Gordon's and Adams' Landings on the west and on the Vermont side by Sand Bar Bridge. Hotels and farm houses furnish accommodation at from $7.00 a week upward.

GORDON'S LANDING is owned by D. I. Center. About 18 guests are provided for in the large stone house here, Post Office, Pearl, Vt. Entertainment can be had in the southerly portion of the island as follows: (Post Office address, South Hero, Vt.)

"Iodine Spring House," Capt. Warren Corbin, proprietor, on Keeler's Bay. Capacity about 50. Rates, $2 per day; $7 to $10 per week. Open all the year. Distance 3½ miles from Gordon's Landing. "Island House," C. S. Keeler, proprietor. P. O., South Hero. Capacity 20. Rates, $2 per day; $8 to $10 per week; four miles from Gordon's, fare $1. "Locust Grove," H. Kibbe, proprietor.

Capacity about 30; to Gordon's six miles. "Martin Brothers" are near Locust Grove, with accommodations for about a dozen.

Eagle Camp on Rockwell's Bay is the summer place of Prof. George W. Perry, State Geologist, of Rutland, Vt., who brings a class of his boys here annually for summer outing.

ADAMS' LANDING. Adams House will provide for about 20 guests at $2 per day; $8 to $10 per week. Open June to October. Edwin Adams, proprietor. P. O. address, Adams, Vt.

LADD'S LANDING is at the northern extremity of the island. Alfred Ladd will provide for 15 guests; Mrs. Julia Childs for 12. P. O., Grand Isle, Vt.

NORTH HERO extends northerly from South Hero, to which it is connected at Ladd's, by a swing bridge. The post office is North Hero, on the east side of the island about four miles from its south end. Steamer lands regularly through the summer. Boarding houses are as follows: Mrs. C. E. Darrow, on Hubbard's Bay 1½ miles north of Bow and Arrow Point; Mrs. H. W. Allen at the hamlet of North Hero; $1.25 per day, $6 per week. Open June 1st to October, with capacity for about 30; Nicholas Hale near by with accommodations for ten or a dozen; Mrs. Ruth McBride on the east shore, three miles north of the steamboat landing, will take care of 12, at about $6 per week. Open June to September; J. N. Parker will provide for 12 a half mile further north, at $1 per day, $6 per week. 25 cents per meal. Capacity 6 to 10. Open June 1st to October.

ISLE LAMOTTE is 9 miles north of Cumberland Head. It is 5½ miles long by about 1½ wide.

About its southern extremity are valuable black marble quarries. On its west shore, midway, is the site of a fort, built in 1812, and near its north end the ruins of Fort St. Anne, built in 1866. The post office, located centrally, is Isle LaMotte, Vt. Communication with the New York shore is had by ferry to Chazy Landing and to Alburgh Tongue by bridge at the north end.

The Island House is here, midway of the island, where the road runs to the four points of the compass. Capacity 15. Rates, $1.50 per day; $7.00 to $12 per week. Open all the year. H. H. Hill, proprietor. Stage from Alburgh Station, 6 miles, 50 cents. Summer boarders are also taken at the houses of E. S. Fleury and N. W. Fisk, on the west side, and Cyrus Holbrook, N. G. Hill and M. Phelps, on the east side, in the southerly part of the island. At the northern part, on the west, doors are thrown open by D. T. Trombly, M. Carron, Wm. H. Yale and Wm. F. Hill, the last at the light-house, while the east side, north, is represented by the houses of C. G. & E. S. Holcomb and W. D. Osborn—all of which address at Isle LaMotte, Vt.

ALBURGH SPRINGS is near the east shore of Alburgh Tongue, a mile north of Alburgh Station, seven miles east of Rouse's Point. Its sulphur and lithia springs attract visitors who bathe in, and drink the waters. Hotels are the Alburgh Springs House and the Mansion House. Rates, $2.50 to $3 per day.

THE GREAT BACK BAY is a revelation. It might remain undiscovered for years by the voyager through from north or south if not especially sought for. It is revealed in its broad beauty and entirety only from the hills that compass it about on the east. Glance at the map and you will note that it forms by considerable the larger body of the lake at its north end. It is entered through the narrow passage between North and South Hero Islands or through the long, slim passage at the north. Away at the south it stretches, cut across, finally by Sand-Bar Bridge; at the north the open water is dotted with numerous small islands; east, St. Albans Bay enters deep into the main land, flanked and guarded by outstretching points and islands. This is noted fishing water and its shores favorite camping grounds. Some of these camps are for hire and some go only by favor.

CAMP WATSON is one of the last. It is an ideal summer camp on an extensive scale, where Hiram Atkins, Editor-in-chief of the "Argus and Patriot" of Montpelier, Vt., entertains his friends in royal American style. It consists of a large central cottage containing the dining-room, library and four sleeping rooms used in the cool early and late days of the season; flanked during July and August by a long line of tents that suggests soldier life in earnest. At this time two cooks and three or four table girls and four boatmen are required to keep matters moving. Fifty people are often in camp, and such is the power of the Atkins eye that they usually retire at 10 o'clock evenings, and from that time until 6:30 of the morning refrain from any excess of noise or boisterous conduct, and attend regular Episcopal services on the Sabbath, the last, however, enforced by a penalty too horrible for the average camper, with the average camper's appetite—and thirst—to contemplate for a moment. Camp Watson has been established twenty years. May it stand a hundred.

Camps along this shore to let are owned respectively by Zeb. Everest, Aldis Martin and Charles Rich. Summer boarders are taken by W. B. Halbert, George Youngers and A. Lazelle and Rocky Point Hotel, on St. Albans Point. Address at St. Albans Bay.

St. Albans is a characteristic Yankee town, having a more cosmopolitan air, however, than most New England villages, due largely to the fact that the large construction and repair shops of the Central Vermont R. R. are located here. The lower part of the town, in the vicinity of the railway station, is level; but the land soon rises, and the principal business street, with the pleasantest part of the town, is built upon a gently sloping hill overlooking Lake Champlain, 2½ miles distant. A spacious park emphasizes the focal part of the town. It is spangled with pathways leading beneath fine elms almost as dense and stately as those of the storied aisles of classic New Haven. The Welden is the chief hotel of the town. Rates not given. J. C. Finch, proprietor.

Aldis Hill, an elevation near the town commands the ranges of the Adirondacks and Green Mountains, and a wide stretch of Lake Champlain. The ride to Bellevue, a winding hillside road, leading to the top of a neighboring eminence, gives one of the most extensive views in the State.

Samson's Lake View House is on the lake shore three miles north of St. Albans Point. P. O., Lake View House, Vt., H. L. Samson, proprietor. Capacity of house 50. Rates, $2 per day; $10 to $12 per week.

HOTEL CHAMPLAIN, of the east, is at the north end of the "Great Back Bay" locally known as Maquam, the western terminus of the St. J. & L. C. R. R. Close connections are made at Swanton with trains for Boston and New York. Excellent fishing is found here, yielding small mouthed black bass, pickerel, pike and muscallonge. Fishing boats, experienced guides and all necessaries for sport can be had here during the fishing season. Pleasant drives lead back into the country and south along the lake shore. This is the original " Hotel Champlain" and not to be confounded with its new neighbor on the west shore. Rates, $2.50 per day; $9 to $14 per week. Open June 1st. C. F. Smith, proprietor. P. O., Maquam, Vt. Telegraph office in the house.

Continuing northward around Hog Island (made an island by the united waters of Maquam and Charcoal Creeks) the spreading delta of the Missisquoi River is found where the "Swanton Gun Club" go regularly into camp. From this point is seen the noble expanse of Missisquoi Bay, 4 miles wide and extending down into the dominion of Canada an equal distance.

HIGHGATE SPRINGS is on the shore of the bay, backward southeast from the Delta. It is 14 miles north of St. Albans and about two miles south of the Canada line. The Franklin House and cottages standing here furnish excellent accommodations for 150 guests. Judson L. Scott, proprietor. Board $2.50 to $3.00 per day; $10.00 to $20.00 per week. Open from June 1st to October. Post and telegraph offices in the house. The attractions are duck-hunting and fishing. The place is attractive, the fare and accommodations excellent, and the mineral water—ah, that water! it should be tasted to be appreciated. It has been analyzed and the man survived! Anyway, the spring houses look nice in a picture.

MISSISQUOI PARK is a few rods north of the station on the shore of Missisquoi Bay. Nature has been lavish of her favors here. The grounds are broken into delightful forms, shaded by far spreading butternuts, elms—graceful as weeping willows—and cedars, twisted and shaggy. Velvety sward and richly colored rocks and ledges, cropping out, complete the picture, and the Central Vermont railroad has enhanced its beauties by making its enjoyment possible. It has encouraged Nature by building cozy seats through Lovers' Lane, and opening up secluded walks under the trees. It has built swings for two, of the kind worked by its occupants, with no one to interfere, and it has furnished the time-honored, inevitable dancing pavilion and nickle-drawing refreshment rooms. On the whole, the place is delightful, and is appreciated by the immense excursions that come from the north, south and east to enjoy its favors.

And here we must say good-bye, and—whether your course leads westward to the sparking waters that mirror the Thousand Islands; to the splendors that cluster around Mount Royal; to the quaint places of Quebec, or eastward, to where you lose yourself among the mighty fastnesses of the White Hills of New Hampshire—wish you many happy seasons yet to come and "*Bon voyage.*"

Index to Advertisements.

Alphabetically arranged.

HOTELS.—Adirondacks, Miller's Saranac Lake H. 160 ; St. Hubert's Inn, 159. **Albany,** Hotel Kenmore, 171. **Glens Falls,** Rockwell House, 151. **Lake Champlain,** Cumberland House, 151 ; Hotel Champlain, 167. **Lake George,** Central House, 155 ; Hundred Island, 158 ; Island Harbor, 157 ; Kattskill, 155 ; Lake House, 155 ; Lake View, 157 ; Mohican, 156 ; Sagamore, 157 ; Trout House, 157 ; Trout Pavilion, 155. **Ticonderoga,** Burleigh House, 158. **Saratoga,** Saratoga department of this book, Albemarle, 47 ; Clarendon, 47 ; Columbian, 47 ; Congress Hall, 47 ; Elmwood Hall, 46 ; Dr. Hamilton's, 46 ; Dr. Strong's, 48 ; Huestis House, 47 ; Spencer House, 46 ; United States, 46 ; Windsor, 47 ; Woodbridge Hall, 47 ; Worden, 46.

RAILROADS.—Chateaugay, 174. Delaware & Hudson, 173. Fitchburg, 175. New York Central & Hudson River, 172.

STEAMBOATS.—Citizens' Evening Line, 152 ; Hudson River Day Boats, inside cover, Saratoga side of book ; People's Line, page 48, Saratoga side of book ; Lake George and Lake Champlain, 153.

GLENS FALLS.—Hotel, 151 ; Insurance Company, 150 ; Livery, 149 ; Photographer, 150 ; Shirts, Collars and Cuffs, 150-151 ; Terra Cotta and Brick Co., 150 ; Business Cards, 147-151.

LAKE GEORGE.—Business Cards, 154 ; Books and Pictures, 157 ; Drug Store, 154 ; L. G. A., 155 ; "Lake George Mirror," 154.

PHOTOGRAPHIC Outfits and Publications.—Eastman's Kodak Company, 169 ; J. H. McDonald, 48 (Saratoga Department) ; Photo-Gravure Co., 152.

BOOKS and PERIODICALS.—Adirondacks, 149 ; Forest and Stream, 168 ; Sun and Shade, 152.

MAPS.—Adirondack Wilderness, 146-168, and inside front cover ; Lake Champlain, 149-169.

INSURANCE.—New York Life, 170.

CONGRESS WATER, 49, Saratoga side.

MAPS, BOOKS AND PHOTOGRAPHS,

PUBLISHED BY S. R. STODDARD, GLENS FALLS, N. Y.

GUIDE BOOKS.

The Adirondacks, Illustrated.—16 mo., 272 pages, pseudo-cloth cover, 25 cents.

ALBANY EVENING JOURNAL.—"Routes, fares to different points, time-tables, maps, guides, and whatever else the traveler is most concerned in knowing, are treated clearly and intelligently." NEW YORK TIMES.—"A book that may be read through from beginning to end at any time, and be found full of interesting reading matter." TROY TIMES.—"A delightful book, well spiced with anecdote and adventure."

Saratoga, Lake George and Lake Champlain, historical and descriptive, 16 mo., 200 pages, pseudo-cloth cover, 25 cents. Contains colored map three feet long, outline cuts of mountains, islands, etc., as seen from the passing steamer.

MAPS.—**Map of the Adirondack Wilderness.** Pocket edition on map-bond paper, in board cover $1.00.

FOREST & STREAM.—"It is the most complete map of the Adirondack region ever published, and is just what is wanted by a party intending to camp out." SHOOTING AND FISHING.—"State officials consult it and the Fish Commissioners depend upon it for use of the State Game Protectors."

Map of Lake George. Scale 1 mile to an inch. Pocket edition on map-bond paper, board cover 50 cents.

Map of Lake Champlain. Scale 2½ miles to an inch, with smaller maps of the Richelieu River, and routes and distances to important points. Pocket edition on map-bond paper, board cover, 50cts.

BOOKS OF PICTURES.

Lake George. Twelve photogravure plates 10x12 inches, comprising over 50 choice bits of Lake George scenery. Bound in torchon board, with illuminated title, $1.50. **Among the Mountains of the Adirondacks.**—Ten plates. Same style and size as Lake George, $1.50. **Through the Lake Country of the Adirondacks.**—Same as above, $1.50. **The Hudson River, from its Source to the Sea**—Same as above $1.50. **Au Sable Chasm.**—Photogravure, twelve pages of pictures, 5½x7 inches. Illuminated title. In mailing box, 50 cents.

SOUVENIRS OF THE NORTH. (Price 75 cents each, contain from eighteen to thirty representative views of sections indicated by their titles, reproduced by the Photo-Gravure Company. Size 5½x7 inches.) **Saratoga, Lake George, Blue Mountain Lake, Raquette Lake, Long Lake, Tupper Lake Region, Luzerne and Schroon Lake, Wild Lakes of the Adirondacks**, (Au Sable Lakes, Tear-of-the-clouds, Avalanche, Colden, Sandford, Henderson, etc.) **Elizabethtown and Keene Valley, North Elba and beyond, Lake Placid, The Saranac Lakes, Winter at Saranac Lake, Glens Falls, Howes Cave.** In mailing box 75 cents each.

PHOTOGRAPHS of the Adirondacks, Lake George, Lake Champlain, the Hudson River, West Point Military Academy, Howes Cave, Mount Desert Island, the Bay of Fundy, etc. Prices, per doz., Crystal Stereos, $2.00; Boudoir Views (5x8) $3.00; Imperial Views (7x9) $6.00; 10x14 Views, $1.00 each; 16x20 Views (unmounted) in mailing tubes. $2.00 each.

Lantern Slides. Any subject in my collection of views at 50 cents each. **Transparencies** in nickel frames 5x8 inches, $1.25; 8x10 inches, $2.50.

All goods above (except lantern slides and transparencies) sent postpaid on receipt of price.

Address, **S. R. STODDARD** GLENS FALLS, N. Y.

GLENS FALLS BUSINESS HOUSES.
ALPHABETICALLY ARRANGED.

BOOKS.—P. P. Braley & Co., 133 Glen Street. Booksellers and Stationers, dealers in wall paper, window shades, artists' goods, zephyrs, hammocks. lawn tennis, croquet, etc.

Crittenden & Cowles, Books, Stationery, Fancy Goods, and High Art Wall Papers. Oldest house of the kind in Warren County. Business established in 1868.

P. F. Madigan, Bookseller, Stationer and Newsdealer, No. 3 Warren Street. Musical merchandise, pictures, frames and sporting goods of all kinds.

BOOTS & SHOES.—Hartman & Everest, Crandall Block, Monument Square, have boots, shoes, rubbers, leather and findings, with a line of specialties in E. C. Burt's and Gray Brothers fine work.

Long Bros, 85 Glen St., carry a full line of boots and shoes, and sell them cheap. They have the exclusive sale of "John Kelly's" fine fitting shoes for ladies; and are agents for the "Light Running" Domestic Sewing Machine.

Cash Shoe Store, cor. South and Elm Streets. We keep a nice clean stock of Ladies' and Gents' Fine Shoes, which we sell at honest prices. Thomas Thomson.

CARRIAGES.—Glens Falls Buckboard Co., D. L. Robertson, President, W. B. Griffin, Sec'y and Treasurer. Patentees and Manufacturers of Art Buckboards, Warren Street.

Nelson LaSalle, manufacturer of fine light carriages and sleighs, including the combination buck-board wagon. Special attention given to repairing in all branches. 36 Glen Street.

CARRIAGE & SADDLERY GOODS.—J. E. Sawyer, wholesale and retail dealer in carriage hardware and harness, robes, blankets, iron, steel and blacksmiths' supplies, carriage tops, coach colors and varnishes. No. 26 Warren Street, opposite Post Office.

CLOTHING.—D. E. Peck, popular clothier and hatter, 16 Warren St. Men's, youths', boys' and children's tailor-fitting clothing, hats, caps, umbrellas, canes, hammocks, and gents' furnishing goods. Headquarters for trunks, travelling bags, &c.

MERCHANT TAILOR.—Dennis McLaughlin, 141 Glen Street, (2d floor). All garments made up in first-class style. Satisfaction guaranteed.

Rochester Clothing Co., Glens Falls, N. Y. Fine Clothing a specialty. Young Men's Christian Association Building, Glen Street.

Tripp & Ducret, manufacturers of Fine Custom Clothing. Isaac Tripp, salesman; Edward Ducret, cutter, 145 Glen Street.

DENTISTS.—Dr. James S. Garrett, Opera House Block.

Dr. L. H. Graves, S. W. Cor. Glen and Exchange Sts. For two years Teacher of Operative Dentistry at the University of Pa. Difficult cases solicited.

DIAMONDS.—L. P. Juvet. Fine stones a specialty.

GLENS FALLS BUSINESS CARDS.

DRUGS.—Ames & Baldwin, chemists and druggists, 150 Glen Street. Physicians' Prescriptions a specialty. Finest and best equipped Drug Store in northern New York. Mail orders will receive prompt attention.

Ferris & Viele. 1860—1892. Wholesale and Retail Druggists. Dealers in Painters' supplies, seeds, &c., 124 Glen Street.

Leggett & Peddie. Wholesale and Retail Druggists, 137 Glen Street. Dealers in paints, oils, window glass, and artists' materials, tobacco, snuff and cigars, timothy, clover and garden seeds, etc.

Reuben N. Peck, 8 Warren Street, druggist and apothecary. Specialties in patent medicines, perfumery, paints, oils, glass, etc.

DRY GOODS.—G. F. Bayle. Leading and largest dry goods and millinery establishment in northern New York, 139 and 141 Glen Street. Particular attention paid to mail orders.

Byron B. Fowler, Exchange Building, 130 Glen Street. Dry goods, carpets, cloaks, laces, gloves, etc.

Goodson Bros., dealers in dry goods. Sell strictly for cash. One price to everybody and that price the same every day in the week. 23 Ridge Street.

ELECTRICIAN.—Geo. E. Adams & Co. See HARDWARE. Electric lighting apparatus, electric bells, annunciators for hotels, and every description of electric work put in and repaired.

FIRE-ARMS.—T. H. Needham, dealer in Fire-Arms and Fishing-Tackle. Repair work of all kinds promptly done. 19 Ridge Street.

FRUIT.—A. M. Burdett, Groceries, Provisions and Fruits 5, 10 and 25 cent bargain counters, 186 and 188 Glen Street, Monument Square.

FURNITURE.—Chas. E. Bullard. Furniture of every description for the cottage or the palace. Picture framing, spring beds, mattresses, pillows, etc. Undertaker and Embalmer. Monument Square.

Wilmarth & LaSalle, 15 and 17 Ridge Street, furniture and undertaking. Cottage furniture a specialty. Folding cots, piazza chairs, etc. This house having been in business in this place for fifty-one years, is competent to meet all requirements of its customers.

GROCERIES.—J. C. Kelley, 13 Ridge St., Retail dealer in high class groceries. Pure teas, coffees and spices a specialty. Fresh canned goods of every description. Has exclusive sale of Larrabee's breads.

Daniel Peck & Co., wholesale grocers, and general dealers in fine imported and domestic groceries, canned goods, etc. 111 and 113 Glen Street, and 2, 4, 6, 8 and 10 Ridge Street.

John S. Powers, dealer in fine groceries, teas and coffees. Wholesale and retail fruit dealer. Fine butter, fresh eggs, best cheese, olives and table luxuries, tobaccos and cigars. Sole

GLENS FALLS BUSINESS CARDS.

agents for Autograph flour. Boston coffee. 18 Warren Street, and 34 South Street.

M. L. Robinson, dealer in fancy and staple groceries, flour, and provision of all kinds. Complete line of cigars and tobaccos. Thomson's Block, cor. South and Elm Streets.

Smith & Horton, fine groceries, choice teas, coffees, flour and creamery butter. Canned goods a specialty. Crandall Block, Monument Square.

W. H. Stewart & Co. A full line of fancy imported and domestic groceries constantly on hand. We make a specialty of hotel and cottage trade, and are always in a position to name prices that will insure a saving over any competitors. Send for catalogue. 126 Glen Street.

HARDWARE.—Geo. E. Adams & Co., dealers in Andes stoves and general hardware. Plumbing, steam heating, gas fitting, etc.

DeLong & Sons, dealers in hardware, iron, steel and stoves, 120 Glen Street. Gas fitting, tin work and plumbing done to order. Lock Box 247.

Stillwell & Allen, 134 Glen Street. Hardware, stoves, pumps, refrigerators, paints, brushes, etc. Rope and cordage.

HOUSEHOLD GOODS.—N. S. McOmber, 71 Glen Street, dealer in second hand goods of every kind; also full line new mattresses, pillows and bed springs. Second hand goods wanted.

JEWELRY.—L. P. Juvet, finest and largest stock in Northern New York.

Thompson & Floyd, watchmakers and jewelers, repairing a specialty, 85 Glen Street.

LIVERY.—H. R. Leavens & Co., Ridge Street, Glens Falls and Lake George.

MARKETMEN.—Corbett & Callahan, dealers in choice meats, fresh and salt fish, vegetables, canned goods, etc., corner South and Elm Streets.

Mason Bros, fresh and salt meats, canned goods, fish, oysters, and clams. Chicago dressed beef a specialty. 94 Glen Street.

MILLINER.—Mrs. H. W. Mason, Fashionable Millinery, Hair Goods, Ladies', Misses' and Children's Underwear, Hosiery, Corsets and Infants' Clothing, 1 Crandall Block, Monument Square.

OPTICIAN.—L. P. Juvet.

POULTRY.—H. R. T. Coffin, breeder of and dealer in thoroughbred poultry, dogs, saddle horses, Jersey cattle, etc. Address for circular and prices, Glens Falls, N. Y.

STEAM BOILERS.—G. E. Adams & Co., 145 Glen Street. Manufacturers of Adams' Pattern Safety Water Tube Steam Boilers for Yachts and Steamboats.

SPECTACLES AND EYE-GLASSES, fitted to the eyes by scientific methods. **L. P. Juvet.**

1849.   "OLD AND TRIED."   1892.

Glens Falls Insurance Co.,
GLENS FALLS, N. Y.

One of the Oldest and Strongest Fire Insurance Companies in America.

J. L. CUNNINGHAM, Pres't.,   **R. A. LITTLE, Sec'y.**

GLENS FALLS
TERRA COTTA AND BRICK CO.

J. M. COOLIDGE,   **CHARLES SCALES,**
President.   Superintendent.

FRANK M. TAFT,
PHOTOGRAPHER,

Monument Square,   Glens Falls, N. Y.

All work from this Gallery Strictly First Class and at a Reasonable Price.

VAN WAGNER & NORRIS,
Manufacturers of Superior

Custom-Made Shirts,
COLLARS, CUFFS AND UNDERWEAR.

Elegant, Perfect Fitting, and Warranted to Give Entire Satisfaction.
OPERA HOUSE BLOCK.

ROCKWELL HOUSE,
GLENS FALLS.

Capacity, 100. Rates, $3.00 per Day; Special for Week or Season.

C. L. ROCKWELL, - - Manager.

MANUFACTURERS OF

Silk Weft, Madras, Flannel, Oxford, Striped Sateen, and Plain

SHIRTS.

MEN'S LINEN

COLLARS & CUFFS.

Factory and Laundry
—AT—
GLENS FALLS, N. Y.

CUMBERLAND HOUSE,
Plattsburgh, N. Y.
UNDER NEW MANAGEMENT.

Located on Trinity Square. Richly furnished. Every convenience. Table unsurpassed. Free carriage to all boats and trains. Rates, $2.00 per day. Special for extended stay.

CHARLES F. BECK, - Proprietor.

(Late of the "Florida House," St. Augustine, Fla., and "Hotel Windsor," Rouses Point.)

Citizens' Line Steamers.
Popular Hudson River Route
—— BETWEEN ——

New York, Troy, Saratoga, Lake George,

And at all Points in the Adirondack Region.

NEW PALACE STEAMERS,
SARATOGA AND CITY OF TROY.

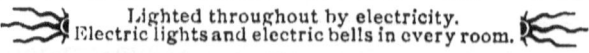
Lighted throughout by electricity. Electric lights and electric bells in every room.

FARE LOWER THAN BY ANY OTHER ROUTE.

LEAVE NEW YORK Daily (except Saturday), at 6 P. M., N. R., foot Christopher Street, connecting with all early Trains North and East.

LEAVE TROY Daily (except Saturday), on arrival Evening Train, Sunday, 6 P. M.

SUNDAY STEAMERS, BOTH NORTH AND SOUTH, TOUCH AT ALBANY.

For Tickets and State Rooms in New York, apply at the office on the pier ; at 207, 257, 261, 271, 397, 944, 1323 Broadway, and 737 Sixth Avenue ; 4 Court Street, Brooklyn ; 838 and 860 Fulton Street ; 107 Broadway, Williamsburgh. In the South at principal Ticket Offices in Philadelphia, Baltimore, Washington and Richmond.

GEO. W. HORTON, Vice-Prest.
GEO. W. GIBSON, Gen. Pass. Agt,
TROY, N. Y.

J. CORNELL, President.
G. M. LEWIS, Gen. Ticket Agt.
NEW YORK.

An Artistic Periodical, Without Letter-Press.
PUBLISHED MONTHLY.

Each Issue of "SUN AND SHADE" consists of eight or more plates of the highest grade, on paper 11 x 14.

The subscription price for "Sun and Shade" is $4 per year, in advance, commencing with No. 5, or any subsequent number. Single or sample copies, 40 cents. Orders for copies of Nos. 1, 2 and 3 will be received at 60 cents each, No. 4 at $1.

N. Y. PHOTO-GRAVURE CO., PUBLISHERS.
No. 137 WEST 23d STREET, N. Y.

LAKE CHAMPLAIN STEAMERS.

SUMMER ARRANGEMENT.

SEASON OF 1891.

"VERMONT," Capt. B. J. Holt,

will leave Plattsburg at 7.00 A. M.; Bluff Point, 7.15 A. M. Port Kent, 7.35 A. M.; Burlington, 8.40 A. M.; Westport, 10.10 A. M.; arriving at Fort Ticonderoga, 12.25 P. M., connecting with trains for the South and Lake George; returning, leave Fort Ticonderoga on arrival of trains from the South and Lake George, 1.30 P. M.; Westport, 3.30 P. M., for Burlington, Port Kent, Bluff Point and Plattsburgh.

BREAKFAST, DINNER and SUPPER SERVED ON BOARD.

"CHATEAUGAY," Captain Baldwin,

will leave Westport at 7.00 A. M., touching at Essex, Burlington, Port Kent, Bluff Point, Plattsburgh, Gordon's and Adam's, reaching North Hero, 12.20 P. M.; returning, leave North Hero 12.20 P. M., touching as above, arrive at Westport 6.45 P. M.

MEALS SERVED ON BOARD.

LAKE GEORGE STEAMERS.

"HORICON," Capt. J. D. Reeves,

will leave Caldwell on arrival of train from Saratoga and the South, 9.40 A.M., for way landings and Baldwin, connecting with train for Lake Champlain; returning, leave Baldwin 1 P.M. for Caldwell and the South.

"TICONDEROGA," Capt. Arbuckle,

leaves Baldwin 7.30 A.M. for way landings and Caldwell, connecting with train for Saratoga, Albany, and New York; leaves Caldwell on arrival of train, 4.30 P.M. for Baldwin.

MEALS SERVED ON BOARD.

GENERAL OFFICE,   GEORGE RUSHLOW,
Burlington, Vt.   *General Agent*

HUNT'S CITY DRUG STORE,

"OLD STONE STORE."

CALDWELL, LAKE GEORGE, N. Y.

Prescription Department in charge of M. Asher, New York City.

This Store may be depended upon for reliable pharmacy, and the high standard of excellence which has distinguished it in the past will be maintained.

Drugs, Medicines, Fancy Goods, Druggists' Sundries, Perfumery, &c., &c.

A Fresh supply of CHOICE CANDIES and CHOCOLATES constantly on hand.

Park & Tilford's Cigars.

Japanese Goods and Curios,
Stationery, Artists' Colors,
Ready-Mixed Paints and
Pure Linseed Oil.

ALL ORDERS WILL BE GIVEN PROMPT ATTENTION,

Dr. W. J. HUNT, Proprietor.

DRY GOODS & GROCERIES C. A. & E. J. WEST, MAIN STREET, LAKE GEORGE.

General Stock of Goods comprising everything needed in Cottage, Camp or Hotel. Special attention given to Fine Groceries. Orders by Mail promptly filled.

D T. SANDS, Main Street, Lake George.

One door North of the Old Stone Store.

DRY AND FANCY GOODS, FINE SHOES.

◁ THE LAKE GEORGE MIRROR ▷

Is one of the handsomest watering place journals published. Its pages are devoted to light reading of the most approved watering place gossip. No scandal. If you wish to reach the best bred people or read all the news on Lake George, you cannot do better than subscribe or advertise in the

LAKE GEORGE MIRROR.

Subscription to the MIRROR, $1.00 for season, paid in advance. The MIRROR is published for fifteen weeks from the first of June until the middle of September. From three to four weeks longer than any other watering place journal published. W. H. TIPPETS, Editor and Publisher.

Address during the months of November, December, January, February, March, April, May, Glens Falls, N. Y.

Address during the months of June, July, August, September and October Lake George Assembly, Lake George, N. Y.

THE LAKE HOUSE,
LAKE GEORGE, N. Y.

Under new management OPEN June 1. Electric bells in every room, terra cotta fireplaces, etc. ; fishing, yachting and driving unsurpassed: reasonable rates for the season. For circulars address

H. E. NICHOLS, Proprietor.

CENTRAL HOTEL,
LAKE GEORGE, N. Y.
ACCOMMODATIONS FOR 100 GUESTS.

Under New Management. First-class tables ; Telephone and Telegraph in the house. Free omnibus to all trains and boats. Finest case of relics of 1755 in the state. New barns for guests' horses.

Rates, $2 per day ; $8 to $14 per week.

S. D. BROWN, - - **Proprietor.**

LAKE GEORGE ASSEMBLY.
PICTURESQUE SUMMER HOMES.

Sermons on Sundays, Lectures on Tuesdays, Concerts on Thursdays, Amusements on Saturdays, and do as you please between whiles, provided you please to do right.

For further information address

L. G. A., Lake George, N. Y.

TROUT PAVILION,
KATTSKILL BAY, N. Y.

Capacity 100. Rates, $9 to $12 per week.

Post Office in the house. **JOHN CRONKHITE, Proprietor.**

KATTSKILL HOUSE, LAKE GEORGE, N. Y.

Open June 15th for the reception of guests. For terms and particulars, address **A. P. SCOVILL, Proprietor, Kattskill Bay, N. Y.**

MOHICAN HOUSE.
BOLTON-ON-LAKE-GEORGE.
NEW YORK.

Address E. B. Winslow.

STEAMER ISLAND QUEEN.
Capt. Everett Harrison
TO PARADISE BAY.

Morning and Afternoon Excursions touching at all landings. Round trip $1.

THE LAKE VIEW HOUSE,
BOLTON, ON LAKE GEORGE

Bowling Alleys, Billiard Tables, Row Boats, etc. Telegraph in the house. Terms: $12 to $15 per week; $3 per day.

R. J. BROWN, Proprietor.

THE SAGAMORE,
ON GREEN ISLAND, LAKE GEORGE,
Connected with Mainland by Bridge.

This Splendid New Hotel is open for Guests from June 20th, until September 30th. It is supplied with a

Passenger Elevator, Electric Lights in every Room.

And all the Latest Conveniences. Its situation is the finest on the Lake. Excellent Table. Reasonable Rates. Easy of access by boat from Caldwall, where trains with Parlor Cars arrive from Saratoga, New York and intermediate points several times a day. Drawing Room Cars by West Shore Railroad, New York to Caldwall, without change. For descriptive circular and plan of rooms

Address M. O. BROWN, Lessee and Proprietor.

Bolton Landing P. O., Lake George, Warren Co., N. Y.

TROUT HOUSE, HAGUE.
Remodelled and refurnished. Spacious piazza facing the lake, Lawn Tennis. Commands one of the finest views on Lake George. Boats to rent, with fishermen in attendance, at reasonable rates. The best fishing waters of Lake George within fifteen minutes' row of the house. We have the reputation of setting a first-class table. Capacity 40. Board from $7.00 to $8.00 per week; $1.25 per day.

CHAS. H. WHEELER, Proprietor.

ISLAND HARBOR,
This House is located on the shore of a beautiful harbor landlocked by nine islands, forming the WALTONIAN GROUP. Is especially adapted to the convenience and comforts of lovers of "woods and waters" and the sports incident thereto. Safe boating for ladies and others of limited experience among the islands. While our rates are very moderate, we remind our patrons that the beauties and benefits of Lake George are as free to them here as at the more expensive places. Pleasant drives to many points of interest, including Fort Ticonderoga, Sabbath Day Point, and other localities which the pen of the historian has made famous. Horses, carriages, boats and guides. House enlarged to accomodate 50 guests. References in all principal cities. Telegraph in the house, Rates, $1.50 per day; $8 to $10 per week. Address

A. C. CLIFTON, HAGUE, WARREN COUNTY, N. Y.

Lake George
"Snap Shots from the Steamboat." 18 pages of pictures, by mail, 75 cents. Address S. R. Stoddard, Glens Falls, N. Y.

BURLEIGH HOUSE,
TICONDEROGA, N. Y.
E. J. WOOD, PROPRIETOR.

This new and elegant hotel is pleasantly located midway between Lake Champlain and Lake George.

The building is of brick, 80x40, 4 stories above the basement. Mansard roof, 100 commodious rooms, **newly furnished** and supplied with an abundance of Lake George water, **heated by steam**, lighted by **electric light**, hot and cold water baths, complete fire protection on each floor. All the appointments are first-class. Burleigh House is within three hours ride of Schroon Lake. Shortest and most direct way to the Adirondacks.

Attractions include many points of historic interest within short range of this hotel, among which are the extensive fortifications of FORT TICONDEROGA, built by the French in 1755, and surrendered to Col. Ethan Allen, May 10th, 1775, who demanded it "in the name of the Great Jehovah and the Continental Congress.

Mount Hope, where heavy redoubts and fortifications were made upon which to erect batteries to bear upon the Fort.

Mount Defiance, which rises 750 feet above Lake Champlain. Gen. Burgoyne ascended this mountain from the north, July 4, 1777, erected a battery of heavy guns upon its summit, completely commanding the Fort, and dislodged the Americans.

Lake George, (the "Como" of America.) with its many delightful resorts and thousand enchanting views.

Lord Howe's Monument, erected near where he was fatally wounded by a French scout.

Fort Frederick, built by the French in 1731, much of which remains in a good state of preservation. And many other localities of interest.

FIRST-CLASS LIVERY connected with the house. GOOD BOATING within a few minutes walk on either lake. Fine opportunity for fishing, where tons of trout and bass are annually taken. Hunting grounds between Lake Pharaoh and Lake George, abound with deer and small game. Telegraph and express office in the house. Rates of board $10 to $20 per week. Transient, $2.50 per day.

HUNDRED ISLAND HOUSE,
R. G. Bradley & Co., Proprietors.   -   SHELVING ROCK, N. Y.

Rates, $10 to $17.50 per week; $2.50 to $3 per day. Post-office in the house. Particular attention given to invalids. Telegraph office within five minutes' walk. Fresh milk and vegetables from Shelving Rock Farm.

ADIRONDACKS.

ST · HUBERTS · INN,

IN THE MOUNTAINS.

At the head of

Beautiful Keene Valley.

ORLANDO BEEDE, Proprietor,

BEEDE'S, · ESSEX · CO., · N. Y.

Open June 15th to October 1st.

Mail, Telephone. Livery, and convenient Stage Service. Spacious rooms, open fire-places, steam heat, pure water, and perfect drainage are all provided for.

Wildwood Paths to Streams and Waterfalls.

Trails to the tops of Marcy, Skylight, Gothics, Colvin, Dix, Noonmark, and the Giant.

St. · Huberts · Cottage,

OPENS UNDER SAME MANAGEMENT, JUNE 1.

FOR PARTICULARS ADDRESS,

ORLANDO BEEDE,
Beede's, Essex Co., N. Y.

CHANGE IN MANAGEMENT.

MILLER'S SARANAC LAKE HOUSE

On the Shores of Lower Saranac Lake.

The management of this well known pleasure resort (which has been under lease the past two seasons), has been resumed by the owner. Improvements have been made to more fully meet the requirements of a first-class hotel.

Large open fire places in office, parlors and dining-room. Nearly surrounded by a broad piazza. 1,000 feet of promenade. Accommodations for 300 guests.

ROOMS LARGE AND WELL VENTILATED.

Single or in suits of from two to six communicating. Electric bells and all modern improvements. The sanitary condition of the house has been improved and every precaution taken to attain perfection. Pure spring water. Connected with the house is a superior vegetable garden and dairy farm which supplies the tables. Trout and venison in their season.

THE LOCATION AND CLIMATE

Is highly recommended by eminent physicians for those suffering from lung and pulmonary diseases. Malaria and Hay Fever are unknown.

SUPERIOR HUNTING AND FISHING

Deer, trout, wild duck and other game in the immediate neighborhood. Trout are abundant in this lake and the brooks flowing into it. Lake trout trolling and fish ng is the best in May and June. Fly fishing in July and August. Deer shooting in August, September and October. Partridge and duck shooting during the fall months.

AMUSEMENTS.

Boating, shooting, fishing, hunting, driving, croquet, bowling, billiards, lawn tennis, etc.

A FIRST-CLASS LIVERY AND A GENERAL STORE

Connected with the house. Parties can be supplied with all the necessaries for camping, including guns, fishing tackle, blankets, etc.

Telegraph, post-office and daily mail (New York daily papers delivered the day of their publication and Sunday papers at noon.)

Terms per day, $3 to $4. $14 to $21 per week. Special rates for prolonged stay.

Diagrams of house and city references furnished on application.

For further particulars address

MILO B. MILLER, Proprietor.

H. H. TOUSLEY, Manager.   Saranac Lake, N. Y.

"The Hotel Champlain"

(LAKE CHAMPLAIN.)

On the Line of the Delaware & Hudson R. R.,
Three Miles South of Plattsburgh, N. Y.

THE SUPERB
Summer Hotel of the North.

The northern tour is not complete without a visit to the "Champlain," the most desirable and convenient stopping place en-route.

STRICTLY FIRST CLASS.

O. D. SEAVEY,   MANAGER.

Sportsmen Never Enlarge the Truth

More enthusiastically than when telling of the antlers the old buck carried off, or of the big fish that got away. But about a thing in hand exaggeration is less easy; it speaks for itself—for just what it is.

(THE WEEKLY JOURNAL OF FISHING AND SHOOTING)

Stands that test. We cannot begin to tell you all its good points. It speaks for itself. You will like its breezy sketches of sport with rod and reel and dog and gun; its stories of camp life, its accounts of tramp and cruise. Ask your dealer for the current number or send to us. Sample copies, 10 cents. Per year, $4.

We will send free (on mention of this advt.) our illustrated Catalogue of best **Books on Shooting, Fishing, Camping, Yachting, Canoeing, Boat Building, Dog Training, Natural History, Outdoor Life and Field Sports.** Address

FOREST AND STREAM PUB. CO., 318 Broadway, N. Y.

The Kodak Camera.

A system which admits of the practice of photography without the least knowledge of the art is presented by the "Kodak."

Anyone can use this camera. The operation of making a picture consists simply of pressing a button. No dark room or chemicals are necessary. From twenty-four to one hundred pictures are made without reloading.

By the aid of the "Kodak" a complete illustrated record of every day incidents, a picturesque diary of every trip, beautiful bits of landscape and hundreds of interesting scenes may be readily obtained.

PRICES, $6.00 TO $65.00.

THE ● EASTMAN ● COMPANY,
ROCHESTER, N. Y.

For sale by all Photo. Stock Dealers.   *Send for Catalogue.*

Two * For * One.

Protection

To family or estate in event of early death.

Profitable Investment

For yourself in event of long life.

Both for the price of one under a contract of the

NEW YORK LIFE
INSURANCE CO.

JOHN A. McCALL, PRESIDENT.

Cash Assets, over $125,000,000.
Surplus, " 15,000,000.

Examine the "POLICY WITH SPECIAL GUARANTEES," and the "INSURANCE BOND WITH GUARANTEED INTEREST."

For Particulars Address,

D. H. AYERS, General Agent,

Rooms 12 and 13 Union Bank Building,
TROY, N. Y.

HOTEL KENMORE,

The Leading Hotel of Albany, N. Y.

*Just added at an outlay of over $100,000
100 Elegant Rooms, Grand Dining Hall
(Handsomest in the State), Lobbies,
Reading Rooms, etc.*

Centrally Located. Convenient to State Capitol and other public buildings.

Free Omnibusses in Attendance at all Trains and Boats.

H. J. ROCKWELL, Proprietor.
F. W. ROCKWELL, Manager.

PASSENGER RATES FROM NEW YORK
- - VIA - -
NEW YORK CENTRAL
&
HUDSON RIVER RAILROAD
AND CONNECTING LINES.

NOTE.—Through tickets to the following points are on sale at all New York offices of the New York Central and Hudson River Railroad. Excursion tickets are issued at prices given in the column of figures under "And Return."

For further information apply to George H. Daniels, General Passenger Agent, Grand Central Station, New York.

TO		And Return	TO		And Return
Albany	$3.10	$6.00	Malone	$9.90	
Au Sable Chasm		14.50	Montreal	10.00	18.25
Au Sable Station	8.60	15.85	via Lake George	11.50	19.75
Blue Mountain Lake	8.95	17.00	North Creek	5.94	11.00
Baldwin	6.70		Northville	4.98	
Caldwell*	5.55	10.30	Paul Smith's	12.00	21.00
De Kalb Junction	8.61		Plattsburgh	8.00	14.75
Elizabethtown	7.80	14.50	Port Kent	7.60	14.00
Forked Lake	10.70	20.50	Potsdam	9.21	
Fort Ticonderoga	5.05		Raquette Lake	10.20	19.50
Glens Falls	4.80	8.80	Riverside	5.70	10.50
Gouveneur	8.21		Rome	5.30	
Lake Placid:			Rouse's Point	8.70	15.35
via Plattsburg & Chateaugay R. R.	11.60	22.35	Saratoga	4.20	7.50
			Saranac Inn	12.85	22.00
Lake George*	5.55	10.30	Saranac Lake (lower)	11.35	20.40
Through and return via Ticonderoga		12.65	Schroon Lake	7.45	14.00
			Troy	3.15	
Loon Lake	10.90	19.55	Westport	6.81	12.25
Lake Luzerne(Hadley)	4.86	8.80			

*During the season a Special Excursion Ticket is issued for $3.50 good on Saturday to Caldwell, and return following night.

☀THE☀

Delaware & Hudson
RAILROAD

TO THE

ADIRONDACK MOUNTAINS,
MONTREAL, QUEBEC,

Lake George, Lake Champlain, Au Sable Chasm, Saratoga, Round Lake, Howe's Cave, Sharon Springs, Cooperstown and the

CELEBRATED GRAVITY RAILROAD, between Carbondale and Honesdale, Pa.,

67 miles shorter than any other line, between New York, Albany or Troy to the **St. Regis Lakes**.

✢✢✢✢✢✢✢✢

ONLY AN HOUR'S STAGE RIDE TO LAKE PLACID.

The completion of the Chateaugay R. R. from Plattsburgh to Saranac Lake, opens up the very heart of the ADIRONDACK MOUNTAINS to direct RAIL COMMUNICATION.

✢✢✢✢✢✢✢✢

Low Price Excursion Tickets

To all the famous Adirondack, Lake George and Lake Champlain resorts are on sale at the Company's offices, Albany, Troy and Saratoga, during the season of pleasure travel.

H. C. YOUNG,
SECOND VICE-PRESIDENT.

J. W. BURDICK,
GENERAL PASSENGER AGENT,
ALBANY, N. Y.

1892. — THE — **1892.**

CHATEAUGAY RAILROAD

— BETWEEN —

PLATTSBURGH AND SARANAC LAKE,

The Short All-Rail Line to the

Adirondack ❋ Mountains,

— IN CONNECTION WITH THE —

DELAWARE AND HUDSON R. R.

— THE ONLY LINE TO —

CRAZY, CHATEAUGAY AND SARANAC LAKES AND LAKE PLACID.

Only Eight Mile Stage Ride,   Saranac Lake to Lake Placid.

Drawing Room Cars on all Trains

Wagner Palace Sleeping Cars on all Night Trains, and Wagner Drawing Room Cars on all Day Trains between

NEW YORK AND PLATTSBURGH.

TICKETS, SLEEPING and DRAWING ROOM CAR ACCOMMODATIONS, and BAGGAGE CHECKED from the PROMINENT HOTELS.

A. L. INMAN,   M. L. FRENCH, Supt.,
Gen'l Manager.   Plattsburgh, N. Y.

The Fitchburg Railroad,

HOOSAC TUNNEL ROUTE,

IS

36 Miles Shorter

Than any other line from

SARATOGA

TO

Boston, Worcester,

Seaside Resorts, and all points East.

DURING JULY, AUGUST AND SEPTEMBER, THE

SARATOGA SPECIALS

Comprised of

Parlor Cars, Coaches, Smoking and Baggage Cars will be run daily (except Sundays) through from Saratoga to Boston without change, leaving Saratoga about 9.30 A. M. and 1.00 P. M. arriving at Boston about 4.00 and 6.30 P. M., giving patrons a delightful ride through the

Beautiful Deerfield Valley.

Further particulars, tickets, time tables, seats in parlor car, etc., etc., can be obtained at 369 Broadway or Lake Avenue Station, Saratoga, or by addressing

J. R. WATSON, G. P. A.

Boston, Mass.

Congress Water.

THIS FAMOUS WATER being now (by a most elaborate re-tubing) restored to all its former strength and excellence, the great mineral-water-drinking public might have been seen the past season at Saratoga hurrying to slake their thirst at this *healthful fountain*, because of its efficacy, purity and acknowledged sanitary properties. While the water is now as strongly cathartic as at any period since its discovery—one hundred years ago—it still retains the *delicious flavor and smooth cathartic action* that has always been characteristic of this famous water.

New Analysis of Congress Spring Water.

Made after re-tubing in 1891.

By **LEVERETT MEARS, Ph. D.,**   -   Prof. of Chemistry.

Williams College Chemical Laboratory,
Mass., Feb. 10, 1892.

Grains in one U. S. Gallon.	Grains,
Chloride of Sodium	550.852
Chloride of Potassium	26.134
Bromide of Sodium	9.653
Bicarbonate of Soda	10.951
Bicarbonate of Magnesia	138.114
Bicarbonate of Lime	149.820
Bicarbonate of Lithia	5.321
Bicarbonate of Baryta and Strontia	0.967
Bicarbonate of Iron	0.734
Iodide of Sodium	0.243
Sulphate of Potassa	0.457
Silica	0.671
Alumina	0.046
Total	**893.963**

Carbonic Acid Gas, 536.8 cubic inches.

In entering on its *second century* and after the *late effectual re-tubing,* we are in receipt of (in an ordinary business way,) the following testimonial from a well-known merchant of Rhode Island.

Providence, R. I., December 23, 1891.

CONGRESS SPRING CO.,

    Gents: Enclosed please find check for $—— ——. I thank you for your Strong Circular. *The water deserves it. It is like the Congress of 1839, when it saved my life, and made me a strong advocate of Saratoga.*   *Most sincerely yours,*

                         JAMES H. READ.

ADDRESS:

CONGRESS SPRING CO.,

SARATOGA SPRINGS, N. Y.

PHOTOGRAPHIC OUTFITS,

DRY PLATES, FILMS, AND MATERIALS.

The old established Photographic Stock House and the nearest to places described in this book, offers tourists and travelers the largest assortment of goods to select from to be found any where in the State outside of New York City. Orders by mail filled promptly on day of receipt, and the excellent express connections insure immediate delivery. Best material and lowest prices.

I keep a dark room where plates can be changed and developed, and all preparations made for a journey. All the standard plates, developers, and preparations used always on hand.

J. N. McDONNALD,   514 Broadway, Albany, N. Y.

Opposite Union Depot Arcade.

"DREW" or "DEAN RICHMOND,"
—OF THE—

PEOPLE'S EVENING LINE.

You will enjoy all the comforts of good living. Tables supplied with the best the markets afford. The excellence of the cusine is a feature of this line. This is the tourist's and pleasure seeker's route as well as the business man's. A steamer leaves Albany for New York (every week day) 8 P. M. Leaves New York for Albany (every week day) from pier 41 N. R. foot Canal Street, 6 P. M. FARE, $1.50. ROUND TRIP, $2.50.

M. B. WATERS, G. P. A.

CLARENDON HOTEL,

SARATOGA SPRINGS, N. Y.

This aristocratic hotel opens June 30th, 1891. Coolest house, highest grounds. Special rates to early comers.

AVERILL & GREGORY, OWNERS AND PROPRIETORS.

DR. S. E. STRONG'S SANITARIUM,

AND SELECT FAMILY HOTEL.

SARATOGA SPRINGS, N. Y.

A popular summer resort. Open all the year. Table and appointments first-class. All the best remedial appliances. NEW IN 1891, Reception Hall, Hydraulic Elevator, Sun Parlor and Promenade on the roof. Illustrated circulars free on application. **Address Dr. S. E. STRONG.**

STODDARD'S NEW MAP OF THE

ADIRONDACK WILDERNESS.

Shows Mountains, Lakes, Trails and Wilderness Resorts.

BY MAIL $1.00.

Address S. R. Stoddard,   -   Publisher.

GLENS FALLS, N. Y.

Huestis House, South Broadway,

28 YEARS UNDER ONE MANAGEMENT.

Rooms large and well ventilated. Heated by steam. Electric Bells. Send for circulars.

W. B. HUESTIS, Proprietor.

THE ALBEMARLE,

W. J. RIGGS,
Late of B'dway Hall, Prop,

ON SOUTH BROADWAY, OPPOSITE THE WINDSOR.

On high ground. Delightful overlook. Quiet neighborhood. Perfect Sanitary condition and appointments. First class fare.

RATES : $2.00 per day ; $10.00 and upwards per week.

WOODBRIDGE HALL, and Cottages,

SARATOGA SPRINGS.

On South Broadway one block from Congress Park. A FAMILY HOTEL. Rates $2 to $3 per day $10 to $17.50 per week. Special for Cottage Suits, according to number of rooms and people. Correspondence solicited.
P. E. STONE, Proprietor. Late Manager, Columbian Hotel.
Station of Electric Railway running to Race Track, Saratoga Lake and Geyser Spring at rear of house.

THE WINDSOR HOTEL, SARATOGA, N. Y.

A quiet hotel of the best class. Late dinners. Music. White servants exclusively. Will remain open until October 1st. Send for illustrated pamphlet to

WILLARD LESTER, Manager

The Columbian, B'dway opp. the new Convention Hall.

Rooms large and well furnished ; light, airy and well ventilated. No dark or interior rooms. Capacity 200.
RATES ; $2.50 per day and upwards.

FREDERIC HEMMERLE,   -   **Proprietor.**

CONGRESS HALL, Located on B'dway and occupying the entire block.

Between the Celebrated HATHORN and CONGRESS Springs.

Accommodates 1,000 guests. Rates $3 to $5 per day, according to location of rooms. Special rates to families up to August 1.

H. S. CLEMENT, Proprietor.

United States Hotel Livery & Boarding Stables

BY ADAMS & HODGMAN,

Division St., (Rear of Worden Hotel.) **Saratoga Springs, N. Y.**

All kinds of neat, comfortable, convenient and stylish equipages, double or single, to let. For Horses and Carriages apply at the office.

CAMP LIFE.

Twelve Photo-Gravures of Camp and Hunting Scenes in the Adirondacks by S. R. STODDARD, size 10x12 inches. Price $2.00, post paid.

Address S. R. STODDARD, Glens Falls, N. Y.

United States Hotel,

SARATOGA SPRINGS,

Tompkins, Gage & Perry, - Proprietors.

"THE WORDEN," Broadway, corner Division St.,
Directly opposite U. S. Hotel.
Open the year round.
W. W. WORDEN, PROPRIETOR.

Under entirely new management.
SPENCER HOUSE,
SARATOGA SPRINGS, N. Y.
Opposite U. S. Hotel, facing depot. Thoroughly renovated, Newly furnished throughout. Open from June until October.
C. P. SPOON,   -   -   **Proprietor.**

✦ DR. ✦ ROBERT ✦ HAMILTON'S ✦ MEDICAL ✦ INSTITUTE, ✦
FRANKLIN STREET, SARATOGA SPRINGS, N. Y.

Charmingly located near the principal springs, churche, and hotels. The boarding Department is well regulated. Rooms cheerful, airy and well furnished. SPECIAL INDUCEMENTS are offered to those seeking health, as, in addition to the ordin ary mechanical agents employed, in general practice, the most scientific remedial appliances are here in use, including Turkish Electro-Chemical, Sulphur and other baths, Swedish Movement, Health-Lift, Inhalation, etc. Specialty of chronic disease and female and lung affections. Lectures twice a week by Dr. Hamilton and others. TERMS– From $10 to $25 per week, de, pending upon the room occupied and attention required. For further information apply to

R. HAMILTON, M. D., Saratoga Springs, N. Y.

ELMWOOD HALL, 48 Front Street. Open the year round House enlarged, accommodations for 75 guests. Strictly a temperance house. Rates $1.25 to $2.50 per day ; $7.00 to $12.00 per week, during the season. Balance of the year, $5.00 to $7.00 per week. A NEW MINERAL SPRING on the premises for use of guests.   **EMORY POTTER, Proprietor.**

SARATOGA BOOK STORE is one of the attractions of Saratoga. All the best makes of Stationery, Staple paper in pads, Gift Books, Photograph Albums, Fountain Pens, Games and Toys, Lawn Tennis, Croquet and Base Ball. A large variety at attractive prices.
C. P. PENFIELD, 410 Broadway, Saratoga Springs, N. Y.

SARATOGA.

As a tonic.—Columbian Spring is a fine chalybeate tonic, gives tone and strength to the stomach, and improves the condition of the blood, by increasing the number of red blood corpuscles. It is useful in all diseases characterized by an impoverished condition of the blood. Dose from half a glass, to a glass, before meals; its use is better preceded by a cathartic water.

Washington Spring.— Dose as a tonic varies from one to two glasses before meals, and should be taken continuously.

Hamilton Spring is noted for its tonic alterative and diuretic effects. The tonic dose is from one to three glasses, before meals; as an alterative a glass several times during the day.

For cutaneous affections.—White Sulphur Spring near Saratoga Lake, a mile and a half east of the village is used for drinking and bathing; and is invaluable in the treatment of rheumatism, gout, scrofula and in all forms of skin diseases.

Magnetic Spring, on Spring avenue, near the High Rock. The water is used principally for bathing purposes, and with peculiar magnetic influence, has been found very beneficial in neuralgic, cutaneous, and nervous affections.

The Red Spring, near the Empire, though over a century old, has not until quite recently, been appreciated for its medicinal properties. It is a very efficacious remedy, in all forms of eruptive and skin diseases. By some it is considered a specific for salt-rheum. It is also useful in dyspepsia, kidney affections, and in scrofula. The dose as an alterative is a glass, repeated frequently during the day.

Artificial mineral waters, are, if possible, to be avoided; as " nature can only be imitated, never equaled."

SARATOGA.

enfeebled, who are suffering from dyspepsia, constipation and disorders of the stomach and bowels, the spring will prove itself of the greatest service."

Congress Spring has long been familiar and famous as a cathartic water. When taken in the morning before breakfast, in the dose of from one to four glasses, it makes not only a pleasant, but an effective cathartic.

Excelsior Spring is noted for its cathartic, alterative and diuretic properties. From two to four glasses is the cathartic dose, and if taken as an alterative or diuretic, a number of glasses may be taken at intervals during the day.

High Rock Spring is often termed the "father of healing waters," and was made famous by the visit to it in 1767 of Sir William Johnson, who was carried there an invalid, and who, after drinking the waters for a few weeks, was restored to strength.

Its chief use is for cathartic purposes, in the dose of from three to four glasses. As the analysis shows, it is a heavy water, and highly charged with carbonic acid gas. It is also useful in scrofulous and cutaneous affections.

Star Spring is chiefly noted for its cathartic and alterative virtues; it also exerts a beneficial influence in hepalic and kidney diseases, and in scrofula.

The dose as a cathartic is from two to four glasses, taken in the morning, fasting.

Empire Spring as a cathartic can be used in the dose of from two to four glasses, before breakfast; but it is chiefly esteemed for its beneficial effects in chronic diseases, requiring the use of alteratives.

The dose, for alterative purposes, is from one to two glasses three or four times during the day.

The Geyser is a strong cathartic water; the dose is from one to three glasses, taken in the morning, fasting. As an alterative, a glass may be taken often during the day.

The Vichy Spouting Spring is the only truly alkaline spring in Saratoga. A glance at the analysis shows it to contain more soda, and less salt, than any other Saratoga spring.

SARATOGA.

43

before breakfast They may be used with benefit before or after dinner or tea. From one-half to one glass is all that is necessary.

Attention to system should characterize the use of these as of other remedies.

1. They are to be avoided in all cases of acute inflammations of any organ or structure whatever.

2. In organic diseases of the heart or great vessels.

3. In confirmed cases of consumption and cancer.

When suffering from a "cold," the cathartic and diuretic waters should be avoided. They have a tendency to aggravate the trouble.

When fatigued, especially early in the day, it is not well to drink large quantities.

Except in very small quantities, and under fully competent medical advice, mineral waters are positively forbidden in all malignant diseases. This may be called the first axiom in hydrology, and completely disposes of all cancer cases. In true cancer, the fatal end is all the sooner brought about by the use of mineral waters, often with frightful rapidity.

As an alterative, the waters should be taken in small quantities during the day.

The diuretic waters should be taken before meals, and at night, and should not be followed by warm drinks. Walking and other exercise increases the diuretic effect.

As a cathartic.—Hathorn Spring, on Spring street, just north of Congress Hall, as a cathartic is unrivalled in potency by any spring at Saratoga, and in this its danger lies. Care should, therefore, be taken in its use. The dose is from two to four glasses, taken before breakfast, slightly warmed. It is highly beneficial in dyspepsia, chronic constipation, gout, rheumatism, and in liver and kidney difficulties. As an alterative, a glass, repeated several times during the day, will be found useful in scrofula and other diseases of the blood. Speaking of this water, Dr. Robert Hamilton says:

"To those whose digestive organs have been impaired or

General properties.—When first drawn from the wells, the water is transparent and effervescent in character, due to the abundance of carbonic acid gas which it contains; and even after its escape, the water still remains limpid. The first taste is disagreeable to many, but after continuous use, the saline-pungency, and delicious coolness of the water exceedingly pleasant. The after effects of a small amount, are scarely perceptible, but if a large quantity has been taken, fullness of the head, giddiness, and a desire to sleep is produced. As the water operates, these symptoms disappear, and increased appetite and calmness follow.

The waters are composed, in a general way, of the chloride of sodium, or common salt, and the carbonates of magnesia, lime, soda, and lithia, with a small proportion of other ingredients. The carbonic acid, with which it is so highly charged, imparts to it its sparkling and exhilirating character; and as a powerful solvent holds the various salts in solution, rendering them at the same time more pleasant to the taste and grateful to the stomach.

The medical properties are almost as varied as the springs themselves. The waters are cathartic, alterative, diuretic, and tonic. Each spring holds the salts in solution in different proportions, which gives to it a peculiar virtue and adapts it more particularly to certain forms of disease. The promiscuous and continuous drinking of these waters, is an objectionable practice, and often results in injury. Therefore, unless they be partaken of very moderately they should be used under the direction of some competent physician.

General directions.—Waters used for cathartic effect should be taken slightly warmed, in sufficient quantity, and an hour before breakfast.

The diet may be liberal, but an abundance of vegetables should be avoided, and only those which are perfectly fresh should be used.

The iron waters are liable to cause headache when taken

SARATOGA.

respond to its general aperient effect. The skin and kidneys are restored to a healthier action, and the recuperative powers of nature are awakened to a strong and vigorous effort to restore normal action. The result is, that the poor worn-out invalid eats better, sleeps better, and gains some flesh, and with the disease still upon him, gains strength, and goes away better but not cured. This is the general effect of our mineral water on chronic diseases and shattered constitutions.

With regard to its specific action in certain forms of disease, I am inclined to think that the various forms of dyspepsia are the oftenest cured. It is not unusual to see the most distressing forms of this disease yield to the kindly alterative effects of our mineral waters, in a very few weeks. Liver difficulties, kidney troubles, dropsy, and all diseases of the blood, known as cutaneous diseases, are radically and permanently cured. The idea that all springs are alike, is a popular misapprehension, although the main ingredients are alike. They differ greatly in their proportions; consequently, in their medicinal character. This fact should be borne in mind by invalids visiting the Springs. The Congress and Empire are the favorite springs for morning or cathartic use, and will hold their prestige, as they are surely and pleasantly active always. The Star and Excelsior Springs deserve favorable mention. Some new springs have been added to the list, already large within a few years, among which the Hathorn and Geyser are prominent. These waters are generally active cathartics, and have a considerable degree of popularity.

I should speak, before closing, of the Red Spring, lately, or within a few years, brought to notice by the proprietor retubing it and putting it in fine condition for use. It is an old spring, but had gone into disuse by neglect; it is a powerful alterative, and has cured more severe forms of dyspepsia and skin and kidney difficulties than all the springs here. Many distressing forms of weakness of the bladder have received almost miraculous relief from its use. It has less saline properties than any mineral water in the place. Its effect on the blood is peculiar and powerful, and many wonderful cures are reported. Its friends have great faith in it.

Many of our chalybeates or iron springs, generally known as *tonic* waters, are used by visitors as well as invalids. They are sparkling, and pleasant to the taste, and are used as a beverage quite as much as for medicinal effect. Our mineral waters have a vitalizing principle that make them generally beneficial. They are exceedingly pleasant to drink and will always be favorite medicinal agents.

DEER HOUSE, CONGRESS SPRING PARK.

THE MINERAL WATER AS A MEDICINE.

T is always best and safest, for those inclined to invalidism, and disposed to use the mineral waters of Saratoga as a remedial agent, to place themselves under the direction of some competent physician, until, with his aid, they have, by studying its effects, established a rule for future guidance. The author having a violent and unnatural attack of modesty when faced by the necessity of writing a learned disquisition on a subject of which he knew nothing, applied to one of the oldest physicians of the town, and one thoroughly competent to advise, received the following reply:

SARATOGA SPRINGS, *June* 15,

DEAR SIR:—In reply to your inquiries as to my views and experience in the use of the mineral waters at Saratoga, as *remedial agents,* I would say that I have been a close observei of their use for nearly thirty years, and during all this time . have been in the practice of medicine here and have been consulted by invalids suffering with almost every variety of disease that flesh is heir to. The most obstinate forms of chronic diseases are found here. It has become the *dernier resort,* the *last attempt* to recover from the tightening grasp ol chronic diseases, by patients from every part of this country as well as foreign countries.

Physicians baffled in every effort to cure these obstinate forms of disease, send their patients to Saratoga for the alterative and tonic effect of its mineral water. Leaving home, and home comforts, they come here worn out, many times discouraged by the repeated failures of their best efforts for recovery. With such a number of the worst forms of disease, one would think that there must be many failures at Saratoga, and that such *worn out* cases would only come to find a grave at the Springs instead of health, but such is not the case. Almost every person that visits Saratoga, and makes a judicious use of its mineral waters, is benefited if not cured. Such is the peculiar effect of the water and climate on weak constitutions. Hope is inspired, the appetite improves, better assimulation is established, and the water kindly takes the place of the medicines. The liver and bowels

SARATOGA.

ANALYSIS OF ONE UNITED STATES GALLON:

Chloride of Sodium.......	562.080 grains.	Bicarbonate of Strontia....	0.425 grains
Chloride of Potassium	24.634 "	Bicarbonate of Baryta.....	2.014 "
Bromide of Sodium.......	2.212 "	Bicarbonate of Iron.......	0.979 "
Iodide of Sodium.........	0.248 "	Sulphate of Potassa.......	0.318 "
Fluoride of Calcium	trace.	Phosphate of Soda........	trace.
Bicarbonate of Lithia......	9.004 "	Biborate of Soda.	trace.
Bicarbonate of Soda	71.232 "	Alumina..................	trace.
Bicarbonate of Magnesia..	149.343 "	Silica.....	0.665 "
Bicarbonate of Lime......	168.392 "	Organic matter...........	trace.

Total solid contents,... 991.546 "

Carbonic acid gas in one United States gallon........... 454.082 cubic inches
Density 1.011
Temperature .... 46 degrees Fah.

The Champion Spouting Spring is on the east side of the railroad, nearly opposite the Geyser; it was brought to light in 1871, by Mr. Jessie Button. The water contains a large amount of carbonic acid gas, and holds the heavy and valuable minerals embraced in its composition in perfect solution. When first drawn it is one mass of snow-white foam (well described by the term "whipped cream"), which rapidly clears and settles in crystal purity. Its strength is such as to render it unpalatable, until the drinker becomes accustomed to the taste.

ANALYSIS OF ONE U. S. GALLON.

Chloride of Sodium.......	702.239 grains.	Bicarbonate of Strontia....	0.082 "
Chloride of Potassium	40.446 "	Bicarbonate of Baryta.....	2.083 grains
Bromide of Sodium.......	3.579 "	Bicarbonate of Iron.......	0.647 "
Iodide of Sodium.........	0.234 "	Sulphate of Potassa.......	0.252 "
Fluoride of Calcium	trace.	Phosphate of Soda........	0.010 "
Bicarbonate of Lithia.....	6.247 "	Biborate of Soda	trace.
Bicarbonate of Soda......	17.624 "	Alumina..................	0.458 "
Bicarbonate of Magnesia..	193.912 "	Silica...................	0.699 "
Bicarbonate of Lime......	227.070 "	Organic matter...........	trace.

Total.. 1195.582 grains.
Carbonic Acid Gas... 465.458 cubic inches.
Temperature .... 49° Fah.

The Saratoga Vichy Spring is under a wooden canopy on the west side of Geyser Lake. It is the only alkaline water at Saratoga.

The Kissengen Spouting Spring, a pipe well nearly 200 feet deep, is on the east side of Geyser Lake.

The Triton Spring is in a small building just south of the avenue, between the railroad and Geyser Lake.

SARATOGA. 37

istic, and] to many, disagreeable odor of sulphuretted hydrogen is readily perceived. Sulphur veins, or iron pyrites, are found in all sections of this valley; one of the most provoking problems of the owners of the springs being to keep their fountains from a sulphur taint, the quantity and.quality of which is not considered beneficial, while it injures the sale of the bottled water. The Crystal Spring is somewhat alterative in its therapeutic effect.

The Washington Spring, located in the grounds of the Clarendon Hotel, has long been celebrated for healing virtues. It is the most strongly impregnated with iron of all the Saratoga waters, and also contains the largest percentage of carbonic acid gas, from which fact it has acquired the title of the "Champagne Spring."

ANALYSIS OF WASHINGTON SPRING WATER!

Chloride of Sodium	182.733 grains.	Chloride of Magnesium	.680 grains.
Bicarbonate of Magnesia..	65.973 "	Sulphate of Magnesia	.051 "
Bicarbonate of Lime	84.096 "	Iodide of Sodium	2.243 "
Bicarbonate of Soda. ...	8.474 "	Bromide of Potassium	.474 "
Bicarbonate of Iron	3.800 "	Silicic Acid	1.500 "
Chloride of Calcium	.203 "	Alumina	a trace.

Total.. 350.227 grains

The Gases contained, and analyzed at the spring, yielded for the gallon of Carbonic Acid .... 363.77 cubic inches
Atmospheric Air... 6.41 "

Total............... .... 370.18

The Geyser Spring is near Geyser Lake, 1½ miles south of the village. It was discovered in 1870, by experimental drilling in the solid rock, striking the vein at 140 feet below the surface. The tube is of iron lined with block tin, 85 feet in length and two inches in diameter. The water is often thrown up a distance of 25 feet by the force of the carbonic acid gas which it contains, making a very attractive fountain. It is one of the strongest waters at Saratoga, pleasant to the taste and very cold, being removed but a few degrees from the freezing point. It is bottled extensively. The water is a powerful cathartic, while at the same time by proper use its minerals may be retained to operate as a tonic.

INTERIOR OF PAVILION, CONGRESS SPRING PARK.

are sedentary, and to all sufferers from the various forms of bilious disorders, it is invaluable. The water in bottles is sold at almost every respectable drug store in the world; the spring was retubed in 1891, the tube penetrating a long distance beyond the point reached originally, and the water coming to the surface now, while containing about the same relative proportion of constituent salts as of old, comes in a much more concentrated form.

ANALYSIS BY LEVERETT MEARS, PH.D.,
Grains in U. S. Gallon.

Chloride of Sodium.........	550.852	Bicarbonate of Baryta and	
Chloride of Potassium......	26.134	Strontia	0.967
Bromide of Sodium.........	9.653	Bicarbonate of Iron.........	0.734
Bicarbonate of Soda.........	10.951	Iodide of Sodium............	0.243
Bicarbonate of Magnesia...	138.114	Sulphate of Potassa.........	0.457
Bicarbonate of Lime........	149.920	Silica.....................	0.671
Bicarbonate of Lithia.......	5.321	Alumina....................	0.046

Total... 893.963
Carbonic Acid Gas, 536.8 cubic inches.

The Columbian Spring, in Congress Park, a few rods from the Congress, is a fine chalybeate water, possessing singularly active properties in certain diseases, and should be taken frequently in small quantities. Its effect when so taken is to strengthen and give tone to the stomach, and increase the red particles in the blood. Full instructions for the use of this water can be had on application at the office opposite Congress Spring.

ANALYSIS BY PROF. E. EMMONS.
The specific gravity of this water is 1007.3; its solid and gaseous contents as follows:

Chloride of Sodium......	267.00 gr's	Carbonate of Iron......	5.58 grains
Bicarbonate of Soda...	15.40 "	Silex..................	2.05 "
Bicarbonate of Magnesia	46.71 "	Hydro-Bromate of Potash	
Hydriodate of Soda.....	2.56 "		—scarcely a trace
Carbonate of Lime.....	68.00 "		

Solid contents in a gallon..... .... 407.30 grains.
Carbonic Acid Gas...................................... 272.06 inches.
Atmospheric Air.......................... .... 4.50 "

The Crystal Spring is near the Columbian Hotel on Broadway. The name was suggested by the crystalline appearance of the water, which does not rise to the surface, but is pumped from a considerable depth. It was discovered in 1870 by premeditated digging. The character.

CONGRESS SPRING PAVILION.
ERECTED, 1876.

SARATOGA.

FOLLOWING IS THE ANALYSIS:

Chloride of Sodium	509.968 grains.	Bicarbonate of Strontia	a trace.
Chloride of Potassium	9.597 "	Bicarbonate of Baryta	1.737 grains.
Bromide of Sodium	1.534 "	Bicarbonate of Iron	1.128 "
Iodide of Sodium	.198 "	Phosphate of Soda	.006 "
Flouride of Calcium	a trace.	Biborate of Soda	a trace.
Bicarbonate of Lithia	11.447 "	Alumnia	.131 "
Bicarbonate of Soda	4.288 "	Silica	1.260 "
Bicarconate of Magnesia	176.463 "	Organic	a trace.
Bicarbonate of Lime	170.646 "		

Total solid contents... 888.403 grains.

Carbonic Acid Gas in one gallon.............................. 375.747 inches.
Density... 1.009

It will be observed that the quantity of salts contained in this water, excepting the Chloride of Sodium, is comparatively small.

Hamilton Spring, back of Congress Hall, is very popular with the villagers, though not very greatly sought by guests. The water, when first taken from the spring, is remarkably clear and sparkling. It is saline and acidulous to the taste, and when taken to the quantity of five or six half pints is usually cathartic and diuretic. It contains:

Chloride of Sodium	297.3 grains.	Carbonate of Lime	92.4 grains.
Hydriodate of Soda	3. "	Carbonate of Iron	5.39 "
Bicarbonate of Soda	27.036 "	Hydrobromate of Potash	a trace.
Bicarbonate of Magnesia	35.2 "		

Solid contents in one gallon................................... 460.326 "

Carbonic acid gas.. 316.
Atmospheric air.. 4.
Gaseous contents in a gallon .... 320 inches.

Congress Spring is the oldest known at Saratoga, except the High Rock, and was discovered in 1792, (just three hundred years after America, which is a good thing to remember;) and to it probably more than all else, is Saratoga indebted for its present prosperity and world wide fame. It is one of the most famous mineral springs in the world. It is an aperient or cathartic water, highly carbonated, of agreeable taste, improving and invigorating the appetite and general health. Its medicinal effects have been tested for nearly a century, and its use prescribed by physicians with the utmost confidence after long knowledge of its great efficacy, and the entire comfort and safety with which it may be used. To professional men and others whose occupations

MUSIC PAVILION IN CONGRESS SPRING PARK.

The Magnetic Spring,* on Spring avenue, opposite the High Rock, is mostly used for bathing, for which purpose it has gained some popularity.

The Seltzer Spring* is a short distance south of High Rock. It is said to be the only Seltzer spring in this country; and it is also claimed that the water is almost identical in composition with the Seltzer Spring at Nassau in Germany. The water is mild and pleasant to the taste. A glass tube, three feet in height, allows the visitor to behold the water as it boils up, the bubbles chasing rapidly one after another to the surface.

Pavilion Spring is at the south end of Spring street and on the south side of Lake avenue, a short distance from Broadway. It is handsomely covered, and the grounds around it very attractive. The water is strong but agreeable and pleasant. Under the Colonnade is the United States Spring, which, but a few feet removed, differs essentially from the Pavilion, being rather flat and unpalatable.

The Putnam Spring, which is one of the pleasantest waters to the taste in Saratoga, has been chiefly used for bathing. The present managers have recently much improved all the conveniences for bathing, and will endeavor to make the Putnam a leading spring. It has been redrilled to a depth of some fifty feet, and the water coming clear of fresh water is much stronger than formerly, and is very like the Congress. The spring house entrance is located on Phila street.

The Hathorn Spring, on Spring street, opposite Congress Hall, is owned by H. H. Hathorn, the builder and former owner of Congress Hall. It is very popular, and as a beverage the water is drank at the spring more than any other, unless it be Congress water. It was discovered in the fall of 1868, during the progress of excavations for the Congress Hall ball room.

The owner claims for it " properties of great value, which have been tested by experience, and not found wanting.

* Empire Spring Station. Saratoga Lake Railway.

eighty-one layers to the inch, and with this as a starting point the following estimate has been made:

High Rock, cone 4 feet, 80 lines to the inch..... .... 3 840 years.
Mixed muck and tuffa, 7 feet .... 400 "
Tuffa 2 feet, 25 lines to the inch.. 600 "
Muck, 1 foot .... 1 0 "
Tuffa, 2 feet... .... 900 "
                                                                    5,870 "

By whom was the old fire kindled? What ages have passed away since its light gleamed out among the forests that covered the now busy place? The Indian traditions of the time when water ran over the rim were misty with age when the white man came; beyond that turn back nearly six thousand years and we reach the time when Adam was a mere stripling and Eve in her short clothes. We modestly draw the curtain and take a drink to her, and the first man who could not tell a lie.

Great pains have been taken, and no expense spared, in re-tubing and putting in perfect working order this old and for years the only known mineral spring at this place. The utmost care has been taken not only to keep out all impure and fresh waters, but also to preserve and retain the fixed carbonic acid gas; and the proprietors now confidently offer it to the public, relying solely upon its merits.

As an aperient or cathartic the water should be taken in the morning, half an hour before breakfast, its temperature not over cool—same temperature as sleeping-room.

As a tonic, the water should be taken cool and in small quantities.

The following analysis was made by Prof. C. F. Chandler, Ph. D., of Columbia College School of Mines, who visited the spring and personally collected the water for analysis.

ANALYSIS OF ONE U S GALLON:

Chloride of Sodium........	390 127 grains.	Bicarbonate of Lime	131 739	grains
Chloride of Potassium.....	8 497 "	Bicarbonate of Magnesia..	54 924	"
Bromide of Sodium.......	0 731 "	Bicarbonate of Soda.......	34 888	"
Iodide of Sodium.	0.086 "	Bicarbonate of Iron.......	1.478	"
Fluoride of Calcium	trace.	Phosphate of Lime........	trace.	
Sulphate of Potassa.......	1.608 "	Alumina......	1.223	"
Bicarbonate of Baryta.....	trace.	Silica....................	2.260	"
Bicarbonate of Strontia....	trace.			
Total........		....	628 039	"
Carbonic Acid Gas.		....	409 458 cubic inches.	

STAR SPRING.

HIGH ROCK SPRING PAVILION.

ANALYSIS OF THE WATER OF STAR SPRING.

Chloride of Sodium........	378.962 grains.		Bicarbonate of Magnesia..	61.912 grains
Chloride of Potassium.....	9.229 "		Bicarbonate of Soda......	12.662 "
Bromide of Sodium........	55.650 "		Bicarbonate of Iron.......	1.213 "
Iodide of Sodium or Iodide,	8.000 "		Silica....................	1.283 "
Sulphate of Potassa.......	5.400 "		Phosphate of Lime	trace.
Bicarbonate of Lime......	120.549 "			

Solid contents in a gallon .... 615.685 grains.
Carbonic Acid Gas......................... 407.55 cubic inches in a gallon

The analysis was made at different times, extending over a period of thirty years, by Professor C. F. Chandler: also by Dr. Steele and Professor Emmons. It shows that the medicinal properties of the Star water consist in the large quantity of Iodine and Bromide of Sodium, being two grains of Iodine and fourteen grains of Bromide to each quart.

High Rock Spring* was the first one known at Saratoga. Sir Wm. Johnson drank of its waters in 1767, and almost everybody who has visited Saratoga has taken them since ; it is an irregular cone shaped rock about four feet in height, built up by deposits of the water in unnumbered ages of the past. When Johnson came, and until quite recently, the water did not flow over the top, although it unquestionably had at some previous time ; but a few years since the owners removed the rock, lifting it by a powerful hoisting apparatus and succeeded in stopping the lateral flow, replaced it, and once more as of old, the crystal stream bubbles up over its miniature crater.

The rock weighs several tons, and is composed principally of carbonate of lime. Beneath it were found four logs, two of which rested on the other two at right angles, and were evidently placed there by some one. Under this came seven feet of mixed tuffa and muck, then a layer of the rock formation two feet thick ; then one foot of muck inclosing another log, and below this three feet more of rock, while there, seventeen feet beneath the apex of the rock, they found *the embers and charcoal of an ancient fire.* As the formation is similar to that of the stalagmite the same course **was** adopted to discover its age ; it was found to contain

* Empire Spring Station, Saratoga Lake Railway.

The Saratoga "A." Spring,* situated north of the Red Spring, beyond the Empire, has been much improved by re-tubing, etc. It is claimed to be one of the most effective mineral waters in the world. The analysis shows it to be very strong in minerals. Physicians and eminent men have testified to its merits in terms of the highest praise.

ANALYSIS BY JULIUS G. POHLE, M. D.,
surviving partner of JAMES R. CHILTON & POHLE.

Chloride of Sodium.......	565.300 grains.	Bicarbonate of Iron.......	1.724 grains.
Chloride of Potassium....	357 "	Sulphate of Lime.........	448 "
Chloride of Calcium and		Sulphate of Magnesia....	288 "
Magnesia.............	trace	Sulphate of Soda.........	2.500 "
Bicarbonate of Soda	6.752 "	Sulphate of Potassa.......	370 "
Bicarbonate of Lime......	56.853 "	Silicic Acid..............	1.460 "
Bicarbonate of Magnesia..	20.480 "	Alumina................	380 "

Solid contents per gallon..656.911 grains.
Free Carbonic Acid Gas, per gallon..............................212 cubic inches.
Atmospheric air.. 4 "   "

The Empire Spring* has long been considered one of the best, as it is one of the most popular springs. It is reached by going up Broadway to the Town Hall, to the right, down Lake avenue one block to Front street, and up Front to the spring.

ANALYSIS BY PROF. C. F. CHANDLER.

One United States gallon (231 cubic inches) of Empire Water contains:

Chloride of Sodium.......	506.630 grains.	Bromide of Sodium......	0.266 grains.
Chloride of Potassium....	4.292 "	Iodide of Sodium.........	0.006 "
Bicarbonate of Magnesia..	42.953 "	Sulphate of Potassa.	2.769 "
Bicarbonate of Lime......	109.656 "	Phosphate of Soda........	0.023 "
Bicarbonate of Lithia....	2.080 "	Silica....................	1.458 "
Bicarbonate of Soda......	9.022 "	Alumina.................	0.412 "
Bicarbonate of Baryta	0.070 "	Fluoride of Calcium, }	
Bicarbonate of Iron.......	0.793 "	Biborate of Soda, }	each a trace.
Bicarbonate of Strontia....	a trace.	Organic Matter, }	

Total... 680.436 grains.
Carbonic Acid Gas.. 344.669 cubic inches.

The Star Spring* is next in order, south, on Spring avenue. It was first called the President, afterwards the Iodine, and is now in a most successful career as "The Star." It is under most intelligent and energetic management, and is gaining new popularity every year. It is extensively bottled and also put up in patent barrels, in which shape it is shipped, after having been recharged with carbonic acid gas, to take the place of that which may have escaped in barreling.

SARATOGA.

The following is a copy of an analysis of the spring by the late Dr. R. L. Allen, of Saratoga:

Chloride of Sodium.......	370.642 grains.	Sulphate of Soda......	1.321 grains.
Carbonate of Lime.......	77.000 "	Silicate of Soda.......	4.000 "
Carbonate of Magnesia....	32.333 "	Iodide of Soda	4.235 "
Carbonate of Soda........	15.000 "	Bromide of Potassa....	a trace.
Silicate of Potassa.......	7.000 "	Sulphate of Strontia....	a trace.
Carbonate of Iron.........	3.215 "		

Solid Contents in a gallon........................ ...... $514\frac{746}{1000}$ "

Carbonic Acid.................. ....(cubic inches) 250.
Atmosphere.................... .... 3.

Gaseous contents............................ .... 253 cubic inches.

The Union Spring is another of the "ten springs," which is being urged into prominence. It is about ten rods from the Excelsior, and owned by the same proprietors, A. R. Lawrence & Co. The water is bottled and barrelled The following is the analysis of one U. S. gallon of 231 cubic inches:

Chloride of Sodium.......	453.299 grains.	Bicarbonate of Strontia..	trace.
Chloride of Potassium....	8.733 "	Bicarbonate of Baryta...	1.703 grains.
Bromide of Sodium.......	1.307 "	Bicarbonate of Iron.....	0.269 "
Iodide of Sodium.........	0 039 "	Sulphate of Potassa.....	1.813 "
Fluoride of Calcium.	trace.	Phosphate of Soda......	0.026 "
Bicarbonate of Lithia.....	2.605 "	Biborate of Soda.......	trace.
Bicarbonate of Soda	17.010 "	Alumina..............	0.324 "
Bicarbonate of Magnesia..	109.685 "	Silica................	2.653 "
Bicarbonate of Lime......	96.703 "	Organic matter........	trace.

Total solid contents........... .... $701\frac{174}{1000}$ "

Carbonic Acid Gas in one gallon.................... $384\frac{969}{1000}$ cubic inches.

Temperature....................... .... 48 degrees F.

The Red Spring was discoverd as early as 1770; and a bath house, professedly for the cure of skin and eruptive diseases, by the use of the water, was built in 1784.

The following analysis of Red Spring water was made by Prof. John H. Appleton, of Brown University, Providence, R. I. The amounts specify the number of grains of the various substances in one imperial gallon of the water:

Bicarbonate of Lithia	Lio, HO,2 CO :	942 grains.
Bicarbonate of Soda...............................	NaO, HO,2 CO :	15,327
Bicarbonate of Magnesia..........................	MgO, HO,2 CO :	42,413 "
Bicarbonate of Lime..............................	CaO, HO ,2 CO :	101,256 "
Chloride of Sodium...............................	NaCl,	83,530 "
Chloride of Potassium............................	K Cl,	6,857 "
Alumina and Sesquioxide of Iron..................................		2,100 "
Silica..		3,255 "
Phosphates..		a trace.

Total...... .... 254 719 gr

EXCELSIOR SPRING

24   SARATOGA.

In describing the springs, instead of attempting to arrange them according to their relative importance or popularity, about which there is great discussion, they will be mentioned. as nearly as may be, in order, according to location, beginning at the north end of the ravine or valley in which they are mostly found.

The White Sulphur Spring,* one of the most valued springs at Saratoga, and which should not be confounded with the spring of the same name near Saratoga Lake, is located a short distance east of the Excelsior Spring, and is reached in summer by Saratoga Lake Railway. The water is used for drinking and bathing, but is not bottled. A good bathing house and excellent facilities are provided for using the water externally. It has been found to be valuable in all of the diseases in which sulphur waters have gained reputation as a remedy.

The Eureka Spring* is a few yards south of the White Sulphur. It is highly charged with carbonic acid gas, and is therefore pleasant to the taste, and by many regarded as the best beverage of them all. Its medical properties are mild cathartic, diuretic and tonic.

The Ten Springs* was the name applied to a number of rudely boxed affairs in a bit of low land now included in Excelsior Park. Until somebody discovered that one of these springs possessed some very excellent qualities, no effort was made to save or popularize the waters.

Excelsior* is the name given to the new spring, and it is now one of the best known at Saratoga. The water is bottled, and barrelled extensively, and is sold in all the principal cities of the country. The bottling house and spring house are extensive and attractive. Excelsior water is used with, it is said, great success in the treatment of dyspepsia, constipation of the bowels, affections of the liver and kidneys, fevers, scrofula, cutaneous diseases, etc. It is a pleasant beverage, and is claimed to be an excellent remedy for the headache.

* Eureka Spring Station, Saratoga Lake Railway

SARATOGA MINERAL WATERS

WHENCE come the waters? Why their ceaseless flow? Where the great laboratory in which nature distills this wondrous beverage and sends its bubbling and sparkling like showers of pearls to the surface, while a great worshipful world of people give thanks for the blessing Various theories are advanced as to their appearance in this particular locality. One, that the fountain head is in some high mountain whose upreared summit has exposed the edges of the various strata composing it, down between which the waters from the clouds are filtered until they reach this lower plain, when breaking through fissures in the rock they rise to find their original level. Others say that it rises by the power contained in itself; the carbonic acid gas which forms so essential a part in its composition Still others that it is nothing at all but a trick of the villagers who doctor the springs with salt, old iron, boots and other like pleasing and economical ingredients which gets up some "kinder of an action"— it is a matter of little moment, however, as to their manner of coming, but every one is interested in the fact that they are there, and Saratoga has reason to feel justly gratified thereat

It would be impossible to give directions as to the drinking of the waters; a person in good health can surround an immense quantity and feel no ill effect thereby; *they* are the ones who are the most decided as to the rules to be observed in drinking, having found by experience just what they can stand — they can usually stand almost any thing. But there

22–C   SARATOGA.

Dr. Strong's Sanitarium is celebrated throughout the country. It is located on Circular street, within five minutes walk of the great hotels, Congress Spring Park, and other centres of attraction—near enough for the whirl, and retired enough for rest. It is open all the year. Sylvester E. Strong, A.M., M.D., proprietor. This house is popular as a summer resort for those who do not require medical advice as well as for those who do, and counts among its regular guests men high in church and state. Among recent additions are a new reception hall, hydraulic passenger elevator, and sun parlor and promenade on the roof. It is elegantly furnished and is specially noted for its bath department. An illustrated circular describing the many appliances designed for health or comfort will be sent free on application.

Dr. Robert Hamilton's Medical Institute, on Franklin street, is an institution for the treatment of various chronic and special diseases, and is conducted by one of Saratoga's most eminent physicians, who has long enjoyed a good reputation as a practitioner, and is a conscientious student of medicine. In Dr. Hamilton's history those admirable qualities, pluck and perseverance, are displayed in an unusual degree by his energetic fight against great difficulties that have attended a considerable portion of his public career, and credit is due in propor-tion. Those who may wish to drink the mineral waters in a systematic way will find Dr. Hamilton well qualified to give advice, while his institute affords a desirable and pe-culiarly homelike retreat for those quietly disposed. Rates for board, $10 to $20 per week.

SARATOGA.

The Albemarle is on South Broadway, nearly opposite the Windsor. It is fresh and attractive in appearance outside, cozy and homelike within, as any house must indeed become under the management of its genial proprietor, W. J. Riggs, long time proprietor of the old Broadway Hall, on North Broadway. The elevated position of the house is in its favor during the heated season, and the quiet of the place is an attractive feature. Rates, $2 to $2.50 per day; $10 and upward per week.

Woodbridge Hall is on the west side of South Broadway close by where the village opens out into the fresh and ever blooming country. This is specially a family hotel catering almost exclusively to family trade although an applicant for a night's entertainment would not be dismissed without reason. The house and management is of the kind that it is a pleasure to command. The location is very pleasant. It fronts on one of the nicest of streets, while its rear looks out upon open spaces that seem practically a part of the open country. The rooms are of good size, some of them very desirable ones indeed, all nicely and comfortably furnished, while the price, considering the accommodations, is very low, ranging from $10 to $17.50 week. The proprietor, P. E. Stone, late manager of the Columbian Hotel will be found efficient and always agreeable.

Near by the house is the general station of the electric railroad which branches here, running to Geyser and to Saratoga Lake.

Contrary to what might be expected, Saratoga contains but few hygienic institutions. Every place almost, from the biggest hotel to the smallest boarding house is resorted to by invalids, while the medical institutions proper often have among their guests as many people in good health as invalids. This comes from the fact that the medical institutions provide exceptionally good accommodations in the way of rooms and service.

SARATOGA.

The Windsor Hotel has one of the most desirable locations at Saratoga. It is situated upon the brow of the hill adjoining and overlooking Congress Spring Park with which it is connected by an entrance directly from the grounds of the hotel. Guests will appreciate the great advantage of such an entrance, especially those having children and those who resort to Saratoga to drink the waters of this famous spring.

To those who desire to enjoy the life-giving air and waters of Saratoga and luxurious surroundings, and who seek to avoid the bustle and confusion of the larger hotels, The Windsor offers special attractions. This hotel serves a late dinner, during the service of which music is rendered in an adjoining apartment. The rooms of the hotel are arranged *en suite* and single, and offer most elegant accommodations for families. Wide verandas on every floor make the richly furnished rooms doubly attractive. The hotel is supplied with every accessory demanded by modern refinement of living, including scientific plumbing, steam heat, incandescent electric lights, &c., &c. This hotel employs white servants exclusively and is conducted as a strictly high class house. Its *cuisine* and service is not excelled by any hotel in the country. The Windsor is under the management of Mr. Willard Lester. Remains open until October 1.

The Huestis House is a large, richly furnished family hotel on the east side of South Broadway just south of the Windsor. Its rear rooms look down on Congress Park. They are large, well ventilated and lighted and furnished in modern style. Some very desirable ones are arranged in suites for families. It has the modern conveniences of electric bells and is heated by steam throughout. The table is one of the best. For 28 years this house has been conducted under one management and has gathered a class of patrons that are among the best of Saratoga visitors, in short it is in every respect a first class family hotel. W. B. Huestis, proprietor.

SARATOGA. 21

the successful general. Mr. Clement is such an one and the patrons of the Congress are the gainers thereby.

It is a first-class house. Rates $3.00 to $5.00 per day.

The Columbian is on Broadway, opposite the new Convention Hall, about half way up South Broadway hill. New plumbing renders its sanitary condition perfect. Its public rooms are elegant and attractive. Its piazza is among the most delightful among Saratoga's large array of sightly outlooks. The prices are from $2.50 per day upwards; $14.00 to $20.00 per week and upwards, according to room. Altogether the attractions of the Columbian are many, and it is deserving of a large patronage. Frederic Hemmerle, proprietor.

The Clarendon is at the brow of the elevated plateau that extends southward from Saratoga, known at this point as Broadway Hill. It is on the west side of the street overlooking the "Pompeia," the Windsor grounds and Congress Spring Park. Westward it extends along William to Hamilton street where a long extension faces the west. It encloses to a considerable extent a beautiful, deeply shaded lawn, within which is the well known Washington Spring, sometimes called the "Champagne" Spring because of its sparkling, effervescent nature. At one time the Clarendon was the leading hotel of Saratoga so far as service and appointments were concerned, and noted far and wide as the ultra-select house of the town, entertaining as it did the cream of Saratoga visitors. It has recently come into the possession of Messrs. Averill & Gregory of the Osborne House, Auburn, who propose to again place it in the front rank, and to that end are using every means that ability and an extended experience can supply. They are liberal, energetic and efficient, and undoubtedly the Clarendon has a brilliant future yet before it. This house will accommodate 700 guests. Rates from $3.00 to $4.00 per day, according to location of room. A free bus runs to all trains.

cess here in the management, showing good judgment in the choice of lieutenants and an appreciation of the needs of the commercial as well as the pleasure travel of the season.

Broadway north of the railroad crossing has a ncmber of semi-hotels and boarding houses of varying pretensions and with prices ranging from $8.00 to $17.50 per week, where personal application is necessary to a satisfactory conclusion.

Elmwood Hall, 48 Front street, just east of Broadway and near the Town Hall, gives excellent board at a moderate price. It has a good class of regular visitors and makes a special point of furnishing a comfortable home for families. Open all the year. The house enlarged in 1891 now has accommodations for 75. Rates, $1.25 to $2 per day; $7 to $12 per week during the summer season; balance of the year, $5 to $7 per week. Emory Potter, proprietor. This is a temperance house, the proprietor carrying his well known principles in this respect into everyday practice. A newly discovered mineral spring on the grounds is of special interest and for the use of guests of the house.

South of the United States on the west side of Broadway are the " Adelphi " and " American," both very good houses.

Grand Union Hotel, formerly owned by A. T. Stewart, and historical as the first hotel to close its doors on the Jew, now opens under a new management. Woolley & Gerrans, proprietors.

Congress Hall, opposite the Grand Union, is elegantly furnished and perfect in its appointments. South it overlooks Congress Spring and Park; at the north is Hawthorn and Hamilton Springs. Col. H. S. Clement, manager. Few men are natural hotel keepers. It calls for attainments that go to make up the far sighted diplomatist and

SARATOGA. 19

way and Division street, and is one continuous line of buildings, six stories high, over fifteen hundred feet in length,
containing nine hundred and seventeen rooms for guests.
The architecture is Norman in style, its Mansard roof em-
bellished with pediments, gables, dormer windows and
crestings. The building covers an enclosure of seven acres
of ground in the form of an irregular pentagon, having a
frontage of two hundred and thirty-two feet on Broadway,
six hundred and fifty-six feet on Division street, with " Cottage Wing " on the south side of the plaza, extending west
from the main front for five hundred and sixty-six feet.
This wing is one of the most desirable features; the rooms
are arranged in suites of one to seven bedrooms, with parlor, bath-room, etc., in each suite. Private table is afforded if desired, and the seclusion and freedom of a private villa may be enjoyed here, to be varied, at will, by the
gayer life of the hotel and watering place. It is divided
into five sections by fireproof walls with iron doors. Fire
hydrants are in each section and fire hose on every floor.
It is safe, elegant and substantial. Tompkins, Gage &
Perry, proprietors.

The Spencer House is just east of the depot, with
an entrance to the grounds on Railroad Place. The main
front is on Woodlawn avenue, which runs straight north,
parallel with Broadway, to Woodlawn Park. This house
is open from May 20 to November 1, and will provide for
about 75 guests. It is patronized by a nice, quiet class of
guests, and is much liked. Rates, $2 per day; $12 to $21
per week. C. P. Spoon, the new proprietor, is energetic
and experienced in hotel business and promises well.

The Worden faces the United States Hotel, on Division street (the street which leads east from the railroad
station), its main front being on Broadway. The house is
a good one, nicely furnished, and its table excellent. It
is open the year round, and will accommodate about 300
guests. The proprietor, W. W. Worden, has made a suc-

HOTELS AND BOARDING HOUSES.

N a volume the size of this, an exhaustive treatise cannot be expected on any subject, nor a full description of the thousand and one objects of interest about town. The design of the writer is to give thorough and well-considered chapters to the mineral springs and the use of the waters; to treat honestly and fairly all objects of *general* interest; and to make simply an outline sketch of other things that the tourist can fill out for himself—as he will in any event.

Saratoga has the largest hotels in the world; the most perfectly appointed and the best conducted. The business is an art in which the most artful engage, and in which wide fame has been earned and worthily borne.

As to their merits, opinions concerning this delicate point are as diverse as the places themselves are varied. This chapter does not contain mention of all, or of all the good houses even, but of *representative ones* of the different classes, and is designed to help such as may need this information to enable them to select the most desirable, until, by familiarity, they gain a more satisfactory knowledge for themselves. First-class houses vary but little in general features. The differences are shades merely, caused by their surroundings or patronage.

The United States Hotel is perhaps the most notable of any of the great houses, and is one of the largest hotels in the world. Its rooms are prodigally spacious. Every imaginable device and modern improvement which can in any way contribute to the comfort of the guests is found here. It is situated on the block bounded by Broad-

SARATOGA.

The Saratoga Battle Ground,* is not so near the village that the timid visitor need fear any harm from the flying missiles, or suffocation in its sulphurous smoke. About the only thing that Saratoga regrets is that they didn't select Congress Park, or some other convenient place for that little affair, instead of going away off to Bemis' Heights, where there isn't a hotel worth mentioning, and fully fifteen miles away. Still, the road is very good, and it should be visited, for it is intensely interesting, and very likely some of the natives who live there can point out the place where the mill came off, or if not, it can probably be found on the map. The facts of the case are these: Generals Burgoyne and Gates got into a fight out there and Burgoyne got badly thrashed.

Livery Rigs — stylish, elegant and comfortable — can be had in Saratoga at rates that are very reasonable, considering the long time the stock must remain idle between the seasons. The finest, perhaps, of any, will be found at the United States Hotel Livery. Office on Division street, opposite the U. S. office.

"The Pompeia" is *not* a railroad or a guide book but a marvelous revelation of the dead past—a reproduction of a Roman home as it stood before fiery Vesuvius blotted it out in a flood of lava eighteen hundred years ago. Among Saratoga's follies this stands a work of solid merit, instructive to the student of ancient history and interesting to the sight-seer alike. It is on Broadway south of Congress Park.

SARATOGA.

Excelsior Park, * the Ten Springs, the Mansion House, thence along the east side of Excelsior Lake, west to Glenn Mitchel and back into the village through Broadway, is a very pleasant drive, covering about five miles in its round.

The Race Course is one mile east of Broadway on the boulevard to the lake, is splendidly fitted up, and one of the finest tracks in the country.

On the ground are the large stables for the fast horses that here compete for the purses offered so freely during the protracted meetings of the society, while the grand stands and others afford ample shelter for the large congregation who here assemble to worship according to the dictates of their own consciences.

Mount McGregor is reached by a delightful drive along the east base of the Palmertown range to Wilton Village about eight miles distant and up a well kept road to the top of the mountain where, through broad vistas, may be seen a magnificent expanse of cultivated country toward the east checkered and lined by field and wood. Refreshments can be had at either the hotel or restaurant.

To the Spouting Springs and past them to Ballston Spa is another drive of interest.

To **Chapman's Waring** and **Wagman's** hills, are country drives of interest and variety.

Woodlawn Park, belonging to Judge Henry Hilton, though private property, is, through the owner's liberality, free to all visitors to Saratoga. It is located about a half-mile northwest of the village. It contains nearly a thousand acres of wood, field and dell, which a generous expenditure of money has turned into a magnificent park. Drives to the extent of nearly twenty miles, rivaling those of the great public parks of the cities in beauty and attractiveness, have been thrown open for the benefit of all, and only a portion of the whole, the immediate surroundings of Mr. Hilton's mansion, is under special restrictions.

SARATOGA.

Saratoga Lake is reached by a charming drive of six miles over a splendid road-bed where the dust is kept down by constant sprinkling throughout its entire length, passing the race course, Lake Lovely and other interesting objects on the way. The avenue is a continuation of Congress street, which, as it passes the outskirts of the village, reaches out into a broad level boulevard, beautified by a tripple row of trees that separate it into parallel streets, where those who travel it, remembering the rule to keep to the right, pass out on one side and back on the other. The lake is nine miles in length, and at its broadest part, opposite Snake Hill, is about three miles in width; it is rather shallow, its beautiful wooded shores alternating with the glistening white beach impresses one with its quiet beauty, rather than any thing like the grandeur of Lake George, or the still wider lakes of the Adirondacks.

Moon's Lake House, near the outlet where the road from Saratoga first touches the lake, is one of the loveliest places imaginable. It has but few resident boarders, the proprietor catering principally to the loads that flock there to enjoy his faultless dinners, for among other things Moon is noted for his game dinners, inimitable fried potatoes, and we might also remark *price*, but as every thing is princely, those who have plenty of money to spend find no fault, and those who have little know enough to keep away, for he is a harvest Moon in the fullest sense of the word, and does not rise to shine for nothing. Roll on, silvery Moon.

A fleet of skiffs and two or three sail boats are at the foot of the lawn, and a pretty little steam yacht lies at the dock while all the necessaries for fishing are furnished when required. Other houses are scattered along the shores of the lake, affording quiet retreats for those who would escape the rush of the hotels.

Snake Hill. † Four miles from Moon's toward the South, is a gracefully rounded cone-like hill, that is the prominent, omipresent center of almost every picture of the lake.

* Saratoga Lake Station. † White Sulphur Springs Station, Saratoga Lake Railway.

WALKS AND DRIVES.

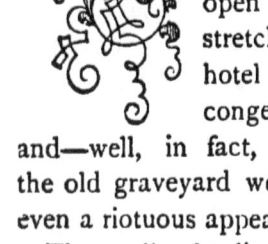HE DRIVES about Saratoga are of vary·ing degrees of attractiveness, and enough for all without crowding any.

A few steps from the largest and most central of the hotels takes one out into the open country, where beautiful meadows stretch away in every direction. Every large hotel has its own private park, which, with congenial company, appears a very Eden, and—well, in fact, with the right sort of a companion, the old graveyard west of the railroad assumes a pleasant, even a riotuous appearance of cheerfulness, so to speak.

The walks leading to the springs are of course most frequented, and some of them, though inviting grounds, maintained at a considerable expense by the spring owners, are the most popular and attractive resorts of the village. Principal among these which, in contributing to public pleasure have advanced their own popularity and success, are the Congress, the Excelsior and the Geyser parks.

Congress Park, connected with Congress and Colum·bian Spring, was opened in 1876. No park of similar dimensions in this country excells it in natural beauty, or in elegance of architectural adornments. The buildings are commodious and appropriate. Electric lights render the grounds delightful as an evening resort. Miniature lakes, beautiful walks, music, a superb cafe, abundance of seats, shade, efficient police supervision, perfect order, moderate prices for everything, and obligingness from everyone con·nected with the spring and park make this perhaps the most delightful pleasure ground in the world. The admission to the park is regulated by tickets, for which a moderate charge is made.

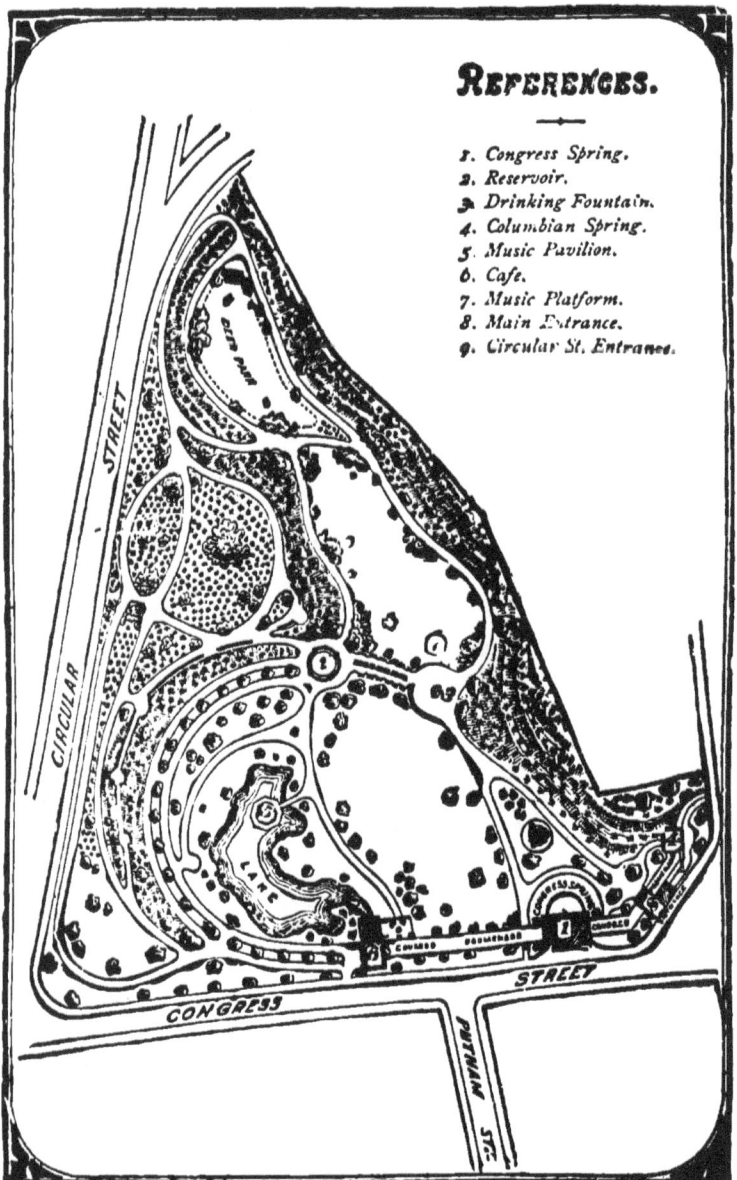

REFERENCES.

1. Congress Spring.
2. Reservoir.
3. Drinking Fountain.
4. Columbian Spring.
5. Music Pavilion.
6. Cafe.
7. Music Platform.
8. Main Entrance.
9. Circular St. Entrance.

CONGRESS SPRING PARK.

SARATOGA.

the greatest running meetings in the United States, if not in the world, are given in Saratoga, occurring every pleasant day from the middle of July to the first of September, and are conducted with such order, decorum and propriety that ladies attend them without male escort. A book might be filled with a list of amusements, so numerous and so individually captivating that the visitor to Saratoga, instead of puzzling his or her mind each morning what to do for the day, only finds it difficult to decide what not to do.

The society at Saratoga is the society of the wide, wide world. It is thoroughly cosmopolitan. The frivolous may appear to predominate, but

"The shallows murmur while the deeps are dumb."

The butterflies may sport in the sunshine—and we love to see them, bright golden-winged beauties that they are, floating on the balmy air and glorifying the commonplace with their presence—but the wheat is there also, and the brightest, purest and noblest of the land who visit Saratoga year after year are not defiled.

"Saratoga society
What endless variety !
What pinks of propriety !
What gems of sobriety !
What garrulous old folks,
What shy folks and bold folks,
And warm folks and cold folks !
Such curious dressing,
And tender caressing.
(Of course that is guessing.)
Such sharp Yankee Doodles,
And dandified noodles,
And other pet poodles !
Such very loud patterns,
(Worn often by slatterns ?)
Such strait necks, and bow necks,
Such dark necks and snow necks.
And high necks and low necks !
With this sort and that sort,
The lean sort and fat sort,
The bright and the flat sort
Saratoga is crammed full,
And *rammed* full, and *jammed* full."

SARATOGA.

the delightful sense of protection from the summer sun that is felt in the great woods.

The Stores are many and varied, ranging from the quaint country combination of cheese and calico to the imported elegancies of the metropolitan "branch." Bargains are often found in the native stores, and voyages of discovery and shopping are among the amusements. In the rounds, C. P. Penfield's book and notion store, 410 Broadway, should not be overlooked. Many and diverse are the articles to be found here. For portraits, Eppler & Arnold, 360 Broadway, show heads hardly equaled by the famous artists of the city.

Amusements are quite up to and in keeping with the spirit of the age, and are worthy of America's greatest watering place. The limit or variety is found perhaps nowhere except in the visitor's capacity for being amused. What is proper to do at Saratoga, and what is most enjoyable, is not a matter of collective experience, that may be collated and pointed out for the benefit of the stranger. Whatever one feels like enjoying, that comes under the head of purchasable pleasure, can generally be had at Saratoga.

If you love music, there is plenty of the best, at the big hotels, Congress Park and other places. Are you fond of dancing? You may sate yourself at the most brilliant "hops" the world ever sees. Do you like the excitement of the fashionable gaming table? There are hells grand enough, and wicked enough, and fascinating enough to satisfy the most exacting. There are the Indian encampment, the merry-go-round, the Circular railway, places for archery practice and rifle shooting; Indian camps, with genuine Indians of various nationalities, selling Indian baskets from Germany, glass blowers and cutters, and many other novelties, to lighten one's heart and purse at the same time and furnish a day or two of innocent pleasure. Are you an admirer of horse racing? The best, most varied,

SARATOGA.

The village, at present, has a population of about 12,000 which, in the summer season, is increased probably to three times that amount. Its principal street is Broadway, of which any city in the world might justly be proud; a broad, beautiful, elm and maple shaded avenue, running through the center of the village from the plains at the south, up the gently rising spur or point of the mountain chain that terminates here. On this, near its southern end, are the principal hotels—toward the north are smaller boarding-houses and elegant private residences. East, along a lower level, is the spring producing section, extending from a mile above the village, south to the Congress, and, although there are a few exceptional cases, the flow of mineral waters is confined principally within these limits.

The avenues, drives and walks about the beautiful village, are too numerous to mention—too lovely to be described. They show the enterprise and public spirit of the citizens, and undoubtedly bring back a harvest through the added beauty and attractiveness of the place.

Saratoga has the largest and finest summer hotels in the world, and enrolls, among its visitors, the beauty, fashion and culture of the world. It comprises, probably, more of the elements that go to make up the ideal summer resort than any other place in this country The village itself is exceedingly beautiful. Taste, culture and wealth have for years combined to make Saratoga a sort of artificial Eden. Hardly anything in the whole town hints business, except the business of providing pleasures, amusements or comforts, to the host which comes solely on the business of pleasure seeking. No factories, mills, industrial enterprises or any utilitarian purposes show themselves to the visitor; but repose, relaxation, enjoyment, is suggested on every hand, and seems unlimited.

The Streets are all beautifully shaded, most of them by grand old elms or maples, so that the lovers of promenading may even enjoy their stroll at mid-day, and with a choice of miles of sidewalk, no matter how warm the weather, with

N 1767 Sir William Johnson, Bart., who, what-ever his other failings may have been, was the firm friend and patron of the red man, heard through them of wonderful cures wrought by the waters of "the great medicine spring" at Saratoga, and was borne on the shoulders of men to where the sparkling flood bubbled up from unknown depths self-walled in the ages past. This was High Rock Spring, and Johnson the first white man known to have tasted its waters.

It was nearly twenty years after Johnson's visit before a house was erected here although quite often visited; then, in 1789 Gideon Putnam built his log house, and in 1803 opened the first hotel, patriotically calling it "The Union." It differed somewhat from the present hotel of that name.

Of old, the waters were used only as a medicine, but as the village grew and new ones were discovered, it became quite fashionable to have some incipient ailment that neces-sitated a trip to "the Springs," until at last people who could not scare up the ghost of an excuse for going, with unblushing effrontery admitted that they went simply be-cause they wanted to, and to-day Saratoga stands the gayest, wickedest and most fashionable resort of culture and refinement, among watering places on this continent if not indeed in the world.

Here are accommodations for the rich and the poor, the old and the young, steady and giddy, wise or foolish, fast or staid, rough or cultivated — all are welcome, for Saratoga is one vast caravansary, every house a hotel, and every resi-dent glad to see the summer's company, for it is meat, drink and clothing to them.

SARATOGA.

The Saratoga and Mt. McGregor Railroad runs from the depot on North Broadway, northerly seven miles, across the sandy level, which it leaves when near Wilton village, to climb the modest elevation known as Mt. McGregor. Trains run at frequent intervals during the day. Round trip $1. Hotel Balmoral and restaurant furnishes accommodations to those who wish. Here stands the Drexel cottage where Grant, the century's greatest soldier came to die, and where he, with the steady heroism that marked his life, fought out his last great battle to the bitter end.

The Fitchburgh Railroad runs drawing-room specials daily, morning and afternoon, Sundays excepted, from Saratoga *via* the Housic Tunnel route, passing through beautiful Deerfield Valley by daylight, and reaching Boston early afternoon and evening. Tickets, time-tables, and general information can be obtained at 369 Broadway, Saratoga, or by addressing J. R. Watson, G. P. A., Boston, Mass.

Saratoga Lake Railroad offers an attractive excursion of local interest and a comparatively inexpensive one. The road passes the "Ten Springs," and branching near Saratoga Lake, runs east to Schuylerville, and south along the east shore of the lake to a junction with the main line one mile east of Mechanicville. A steamer runs from the lake station to the White Sulphur Springs and Park.

The Electric Railroad (from Broadway, foot of Congress St.) branching near the south border of the village, runs to Geyser and Lake Saratoga, passing the race course by the way. During the races cars will run at frequent intervals.

"The Little Red Guide" gives time-tables of all near lines in the most convenient form. It is issued semi-monthly by C. S. Pease, of Albany, and sent post-paid to subscribers at $2 per annum, including a neat morocco case. It can be had on the trains and at the news stands generally at 10 cents per copy.

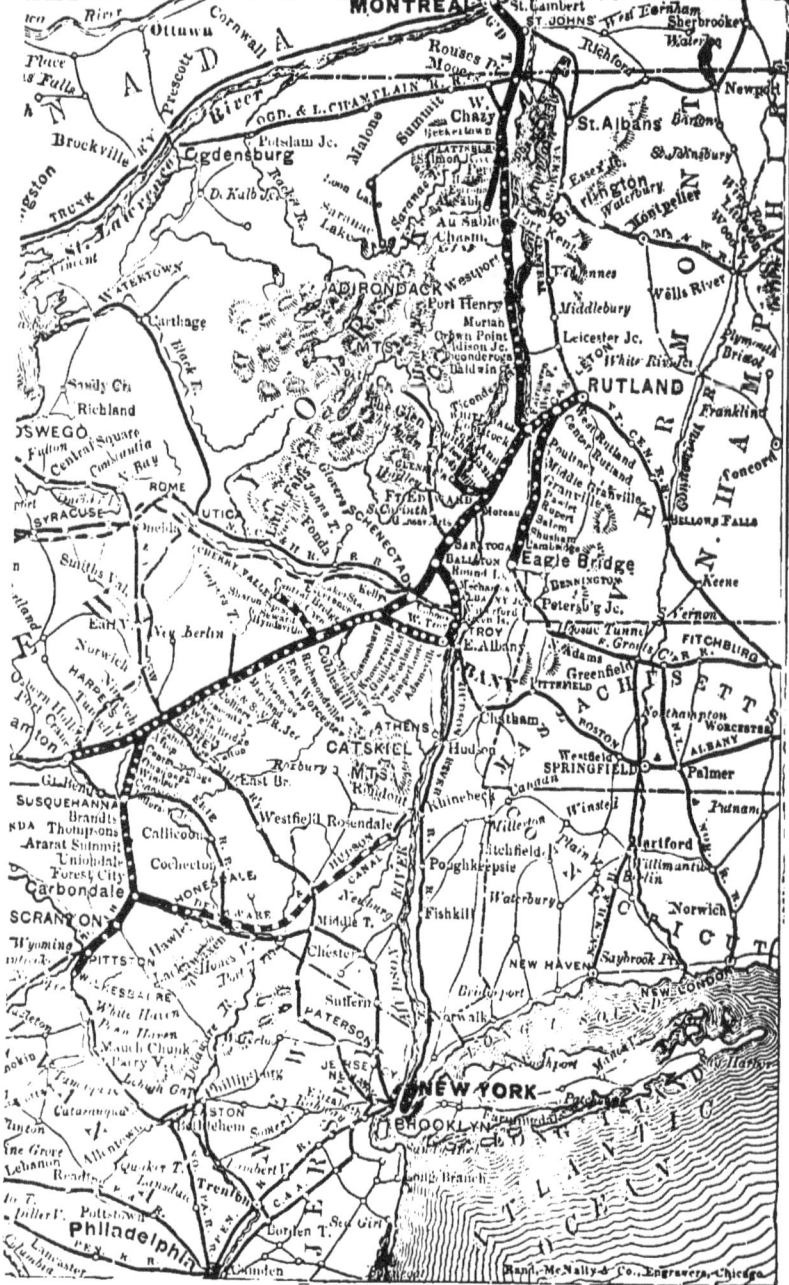

leaves Caldwell on Sunday night at 10:50, arriving in New York at 7 the next morning. The officers of the Delaware and Hudson Canal Company's Railroad are : R. M. Oly-phant, president; Le Grand B. Cannon, 1st vice-president; H. G. Young, 2d vice-president ; C. D. Hammond, super-intendent, and J. W. Burdick, general passenger and ticket agent.

The Adirondack Railway, belonging to the D. & H. system, has its southern terminus at Saratoga, and runs across the country climbing up through the hills to Corinth, thence up the valley of the wild upper Hudson to North Creek, a distance of 57 miles. By this route the Blue Mountain, Raquette, Forked and Long Lake regions of the Adirondacks are reached. Through the summer, trains run twice daily each way, besides a night train which leaves Grand Central Station, New York, at 7:30 P. M., with sleeper for North Creek. Connections are made at Had-ley with free carriages to the Luzerne hotels ; at Riverside with coaches for Chestertown and Schroon Lake ; and at North Creek with stages to Minerva and Blue Mountain Lake. Supplemental to the Adirondack railroad and stage line to Blue Mountain Lake is the line of steam yachts which runs through Blue Mountain, Eagle, Utowana and Raquette Lakes with their connecting streams, affording one of the most delightful of excursions. For matter re-lating to passenger traffic, address the G. P. A., at Albany.

Railroad Excursions.—The principal and most de-lightfully varied one is by rail to Lake George, through the lake by steamer and return by rail. The ruins of Fort Ticonderoga are worth a day's visit. Au Sable Chasm is one of the wonders of the country. It should have a part of two days for comfortable " doing." A visit to Howes Cave will give material for thought and sensations that may last for years. For particulars and rates on these and other excursions, apply at the local information bureau, or send 6 cents in stamps to J. W. Burdick, G. P. A., Albany.

SARATOGA.

little time to spare, or who from choice or necessity may remain in the city through the day, a train leaving at 6:25 P. M., with through sleepers attached, will be found convenient. It connects early in the morning at North Creek with stages for Blue Mountain Lake; at Westport with stage for Elizabethtown and Lake Placid; at Port Kent for Au Sable Chasm; and at Plattsburgh with trains for Au Sable Station and Saranac Lake. For time tables or any desired information address George H. Daniels, General Passenger Agent, Grand Central Station, New York.

The West Shore Railroad will during the season of summer travel run trains through from Washington to Saratoga, without change. Passengers and baggage are taken from the foot of Fulton Street, Brooklyn, and from Jay and 42d Streets, New York. At Albany the road enjoys Union Depot facilities in common with the D. & H. Co.'s roads. C. E. Lambert is the General Passenger Agent, with office at No. 5 Vanderbilt Avenue, New York.

The "D. & H." Railroad has become the most important carrier of summer travel in this country, and is using its great resources most energetically and effectively for the development of Northern New York. Lake George, the most beautiful and romantic of American waters, is reached by this road only, which touches the lake at the south end by one of its branches, and at the north end by another branch. By it also the tourist finds entrance to the Adirondack Wilderness, through all the gateways on its eastern border through which nearly all of the visitors to Keene Valley, Lake Placid and the Saranac and St. Regis regions pass. During the season of summer travel, four trains run daily through to Lake George, and on Saturday an extra train, leaving Grand Central Depot at 3:30 P. M., reaches Caldwell at 10:50. A train with sleepers attached

SARATOGA. 3

The Citizens' Line Steamers, "Saratoga" and "City of Troy," forming the night line between Troy and New York (every night except Saturday), are fine specimens among this distinctive class of river boats. They are of light draft, and fitted up with a view to speed in traveling. The staterooms are heated by steam in cold weather, and are complete in all their appointments. Meals are served on the European plan, in a style equal to the best of hotels. They are lighted by electricity, and have electric bells and lights in the staterooms. Free transportation carriages between the depot and steamboat landing at Troy attend evening trains, and baggage is transported free. George W. Gibson, G. P. A., Troy.

The People's Line Steamers, "Drew" and "Dean Richmond," run between Albany and New York every night except Sunday. They have few, if any, equals in size, equipment, or accommodations, combining all the conveniences of a first-class hotel, and well deserving the name, so often bestowed, of "floating palaces." They are lighted throughout with electricity. Meals are served on the European plan. M. B. Waters, General Passenger Agent, Albany, N. Y.

The N.Y.C.&H.R. Railroad carries the larger proportion of the people who go up out of Gotham to the lakes and mountains at the north. Without ostentation, it provides its patrons with the best of service at the minimum of cost. Special fast trains leave the Grand Central Station for north and west at hours that should be considered in view of their arrival at various points later on. For Saratoga and Lake George, the most convenient, perhaps, is one leaving at 9 A. M., and reaching the points mentioned early in the afternoon. Another leaving at 3:30 P. M., reaches Saratoga at about 9:25, and on Saturday night runs to Lake George, returning on Sunday evening to connect with regular sleeper south. To those who have

SARATOGA.

shores the journey lies is pre-eminent among the rivers of America. The literature of the Hudson, in history, romance and poetry is so familiar that every intelligent American is conversant with at least the general features and facts which have made it a storied stream. To the tourist along the river, however, methodically arranged details, which his reading may not have furnished, may be found most entertainingly set forth in " The Hudson by Daylight," written by one not unknown to fame, who hides his identity under the *non de plume* of " Thursty McQuill." To you who would retain its features permanently before the eye the " Panorama of the Hudson," by the same hand, is an admirable hand-book—a titled and indexed picture of both shores, stretching almost its entire navigable length.

The Day Boats are the " New York " and " Albany " —new and splendid specimens of shipcraft, with iron hulls 300 feet in length, accommodating 2,000 passengers, and claimed to be the fastest steamboats in the world. They were built exclusively for carrying passengers, and are the finest boats ever constructed for the business. The spacious cabins are finished in highly polished woods, handsomely paneled, and are furnished luxuriously and adorned with statuary and paintings by celebrated artists. The dining-rooms are on the main deck, where the traveler can enjoy an excellent dinner, which is served on the European plan, and lose nothing of the view of this most charming of American rivers. They leave New York and Albany at about 8:30 A. M., touching at the principal landings on their way, meet near Poughkeepsie, and arrive at their destinations at about 6 P. M. A pleasant feature is an orchestra on each steamer. Fare $2. During the season fast trains run to and from Saratoga to connect with these boats, and on Saturday night run through to Lake George. F. B. Hibbard, G. P. A., Desbrosses Street Pier, New York.

SARATOGA.

SARATOGA! LAKE GEORGE! THE ADIRONDACKS! Each name bringing its cloud of impressions totally diverse, yet uniting in one common restful one of relaxation from the grind of toil, freedom from the worry of business, the enjoyment of pleasures unlimited,—each perfect of its kind and found in its perfection nowhere else on the face of the globe. How to reach this charmed region is the first question asked, and the effort is made in the following pages to answer; and as a great proportion of its visitors come from the great city of New York, some notice of the thoroughfare and of the generally approved methods of traversing it seems specially appropriate.

From New York to Saratoga the distance is 177 miles, to Lake George 215; and it is safe to say that no public way of equal length in this country rivals it in historic, romantic or practical interest. The noble Hudson, over whose bosom or along whose

	PAGE.		PAGE.		PAGE.
Amusements	10	General Properties.	41	Empire	27
Battle Ground	16	When, and when not		Eureka	24
Discovery	8	to drink	43	Excelsior	24
Drives	13-16	Mount McGregor	15	Geyser	37
Excursions	6	Moon's Lake House	14	Hamilton	33
Hotels		**Parks**		Hathorn	31
In general	0-17	Congress	13	High Rock	28
Albemarle, The	21	Excelsior	15	Kissengen	38
American, The	20	Woodlawn	16	Magnetic	31
Columbian	21	Race Course	15	Pavilion	31
Congress Hall	19	**Railroads**		Putnam	31
Elmwood Hall	20	Adirondack	5	Red	26
Grand Union	20	Delaware & Hudson	4	Saratoga "A"	27
Huestis House	21	Hudson River	3	Seltzer	31
Spencer House	19	Mount McGregor	7	Spouting Springs	15
United States	17	Saratoga Lake	7	Star	27
Windsor, The	—	West Shore	4	Ten Springs	24
Worden, The	20	Railway Guide	7	Triton	38
Livery Rigs	16	Saratoga Lake	14	Union	29
Maps		Snake Hill	14	Vichy	38
Congress Park	40	Society	11	Washington	37
Village. (Frontispiece)		Stores	10	White Sulphur	24
Medical Institutions		Streets	9	**Steamboats**	
Dr. Hamilton's	22	**Springs**		Hudson River	2
Drs. Strong's	22	Champion	38	Day Boats	2
Mineral Waters	23	Columbian	35	Citizens' Line	3
As a Medicine	39	Congress	33	People's Line	3
As a Tonic	45	Crystal	35	Tally-ho Coach	7
				Trout Ponds	15

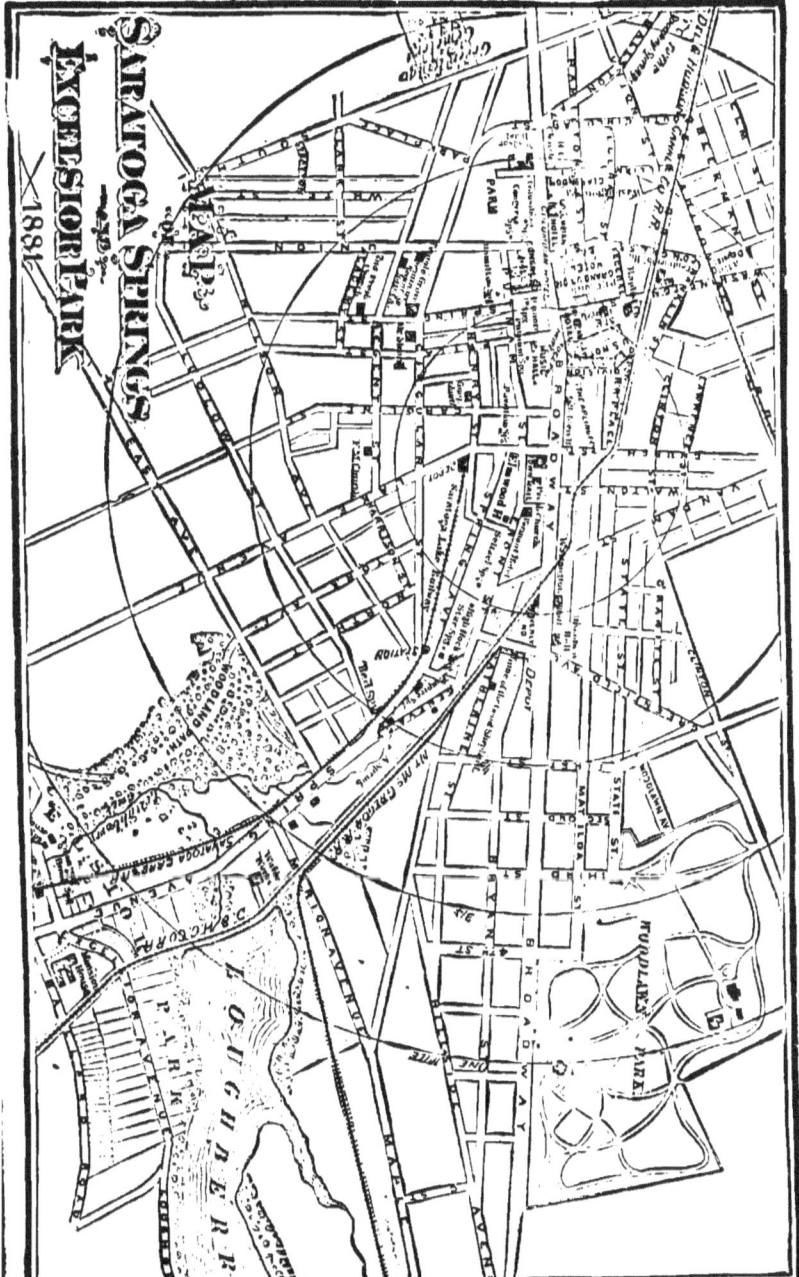

www.ingramcontent.com/pod-product-compliance
Lightning Source LLC
Chambersburg PA
CBHW031814230426
43669CB00009B/1137